THESE SURVIVALS

WRITING MATTERS!

A series edited by Alexis Pauline Gumbs, Monica Huerta, Erica Rand, and Jerry Zee

These Survivals

AUTOBIOGRAPHY *of an* EXTINCTION

]
]

Lynne Huffer

DUKE UNIVERSITY PRESS / DURHAM AND LONDON / 2025

© 2025 DUKE UNIVERSITY PRESS
All rights reserved
Printed in the United States of America on acid-free paper ∞
Project Editor: Liz Smith
Designed by Matthew Tauch
Typeset in Portrait Text by Copperline Book Services

Library of Congress Cataloging-in-Publication Data
Names: Huffer, Lynne, [date] author.
Title: These survivals : autobiography of an extinction / Lynne Huffer.
Other titles: Writing matters! (Duke University Press)
Description: Durham : Duke University Press, 2025. | Series: Writing matters! | Includes bibliographical references.
Identifiers: LCCN 2024033019 (print)
LCCN 2024033020 (ebook)
ISBN 9781478031574 (paperback)
ISBN 9781478028369 (hardcover)
ISBN 9781478060567 (ebook)
Subjects: LCSH: Environmental ethics—Poetry. | Environmental ethics—Pictorial works. | Nature—Effect of human beings on—Poetry. | Nature—Effect of human beings on—Pictorial works. | Climatic changes—Moral and ethical aspects—Poetry. | Climatic changes—Moral and ethical aspects—Pictorial works. | LCGFT: Experimental poetry. | Collages.
Classification: LCC PS3608.U34988 T44 2025 (print) | LCC PS3608.U34988 (ebook) | DDC 821/.92—dc23/eng/20250101
LC record available at https://lccn.loc.gov/2024033019
LC ebook record available at https://lccn.loc.gov/2024033020

Cover art: Lynne Huffer, *Animal Behavior*, 2023. Collage in altered book, with cutouts, flaps, and accordion fold inserts, page 5. Bryn Mawr College Special Collections.

For Alexa

CONTENTS

    I   Fragments Comingback · 1

  II   In the Middle, In the Dark, Between Us · 77

    III   Décollage · 105

CODA   (Comingback Fragment) · 187

APPENDICES · 191

    I   A Note on ~~Method~~ (Training) · 193

  II   Sources (Citations) · 195

  III   Substrate (Works Cited) · 199

  IV   List of Figures · 202

Acknowledgments · 207

but what was scattered
gathers
what was gathered
blows apart

I

FRAGMENTS COMINGBACK

]
]

]

FIGURE 1.1

,

What you wrote, quoting Sappho, at the end of a book, the last in a trilogy you made,
           (feverish)
was the promise of an ending

        ]
        ]
        ] I will go

                                                  (eros growing cold
                                                    after Sappho)

Yet here you are again,
   ]   led   astray

]
by words and the silences they shape. One day, perhaps, you will no longer know what this was. This heat. This cutting and pasting, collaging yourself into negative space: both steadfast and strewn. You will have gone your way
   among dim shapes

ἐκπεποταμένα

["having been breathed out"]
Anne Carson notes: "Cognate with words for wings, flying, fluttering and breath, the participle *ekpepotamena*, with its spatter of plosives and final open vowel, sounds like the escape of a soul into nothingness"

these pages

                                  saying

you, me
petrified bits of tooth,

                    rockglint in gullies
                            (Père Cuvier's archive: paleofossil record
                                      & [you&me]
                                      stonecold human anatomy)

what is black in the museums of Paris?

                    if you're Sarah Baartman you bear the cost of the stonecold archive:
                    kidnapped from Africa for London parade this *unbearable* display for
                          postmortem parts preserved in Parisian ManMuseum jars

          these stonecold fragments dug up from gypsum mines in the Paris basin
                    (*Anoplotherium commune* drawn but never published)
                          in museums, unbearable, fragments endure:
                    poem life overburden (dread, surprise, suspicion, longing) and

                    wish my pussy could live
                    in a different shape and get
                      some goddamn respect
                          one day   jars will shatter
                                                                  in the Musée de l'homme

                             ,

                    : & whiffs of freedom
                    (whiffs of respite)
                          pause at stations of reflection
         saying sapphic breaks [ ] in worldending (Anthropocene) violence

,

A rule for writing:
Don't say Anthropocene.
The word sags from overuse.
Unsay Anthropocene with a (Holocene) fragment.

FIGURE 1.2

Spring 2023. Institute for Advanced Study, Princeton. At the end of her public lecture for our climate crisis seminar, the anthropologist Anna Tsing showed us a picture of a skull. A classic still life: *vanitas*

miniaturized collapse of civilization

A *vanitas* image is the pictorial equivalent of an open landfill where heaps of meaningless yet valuable things are laid to rest along with the worldly values attached to them for everyone to see

Carefully arranged. Bleached bone radiating an arrangement of objects: grasses, leaf bed, lavender nodules of *Laccaria amethystina* bubbling up from the earth. Tsing interpreted the red deer skull sprouting amethyst deceivers as the return of Holocene life in an Anthropocene patch. Psychedelic fungi figuring purple respiration. A skull breathing in the overburden of an abandoned coal mine in Denmark.

]]

[haiku fragments for Anna Tsing]

unexpected things
happened when they left the mines,
left them leaving piles

of unstable sand
mixed with coal. With the mine red
deer died together

where they had gathered
(in Denmark almost extinct)—
herd becoming sign.

But skull doesn't speak
forevering void: unspeaks
last of a species.

          Vanitas instead:
     generations fragmenting,
          returning to us

             as the Holocene,
she said, skull (un)saying these
      newcaught animals,

          comingback bits in
  the midst of our sad planet's
        pits of disturbance.

          ,

Such excitement collaging these Holocene fragments in carefully counted comingback time!
        (sick to death of necrotic Anthropocene prose)
      Break the rules (old jars) & reassemble the shards!

          Anne Carson again (comingback) in her *Oresteia*:
          "Words are coined by pressing old words together
          into new compounds—"
                                              dayvisible
          comingback   lightbringing
   comingback   dreamvisible
          manminded   comingback
                                     dewdrenched
    haredevouring crimsoncovered!
comingback   purplepaved! redsaturated!
                              griefremembering pain

comingback

The comingback fragment endures. Its endurance not steady or persistent,

not a line across a page but   _____
                          _____   _____   _____lines that
                                                                                                 break

returning across a page or a   space for living

          in comingback time   like speech that unsays by saying
    [not the time of madness but the time of unreason]

the fragment endures while the whole crumbles

a piece of meteor
from an unknown
sky

It is the fragment and the fragmentary sta
that are the enduring and normative cond
conversely, it is the whole that is ephemera
and the state of wholeness that is transitor
    Any walk through a museum
        will support that thesis.

what is black in the museums of paris?

    far from paris a desert museum:

    Purifoyed dada junkyard after 66 neon signs

    this creation of beauty from ugliness

,

The Holocene fragment (red deer skull still life) speaks more truthfully (Adorno thinks, thinking fragment with totality) than any Anthropocene whole.   This

       renewed possibility for a Holocene ecology   (Tsing says)

something to   ⎡ in the remains
look for   ⎢ in the remains
               ⎣ in the remains of Anthropocene mining

| in the remains of Anthropocene me my mine- ing |

,

Give yourself rules for writing. How you create form:
Exercises for sapphic erasures or haiku condensations or verbswept weather reports or abecedaries or acrostics or wordcollage.

But forms will be broken (décollage)

Try as you might,
       (or perhaps not trying)
              you will trip and fall,
                    [[

      you will break a rule, then another, even the experimental ones you've set
           for yourselfandnooneelse
                            (newformslikeoldgreekcompoundwords)
Like all broken things, newforms will scatter (let her scatter)

                                    you
               ]] for   rself
                    andno
                                            one
             for
                                            else
                no
           on
          e
                                                    els
               e

remembering   *66 Signs of Neon*
                                         police killing in Watts so hot neon signs melted
                                         more signs in these times allthetime

,

,

breath mark
luftpause
if you're singing or talking
(wind instrument)
take a breath

’
this is not a comma

(respite)

the fragment endures while the whole crumbles

It is the whole
that is fragile,
transitory,
poignant

FIGURE 1.3 Noah Purifoy, *No Contest (Bicycles)*, 1991.
Courtesy of Noah Purifoy Foundation © 2025.

,

Another rule for writing:
It's ok to say "I," but let her scatter.

[she was already scattered]

,

"Wearing
nothing but
a shirt"

she&I

(sapphic)

We admire a text because it

would have
been
condemned

scatters

(along with
Damiens,
sodomites,
witches,
mystics, and
heretics) to

well

be consumed
by fire, ashes
thrown to the

wind

the

like

ashes

to

strewn

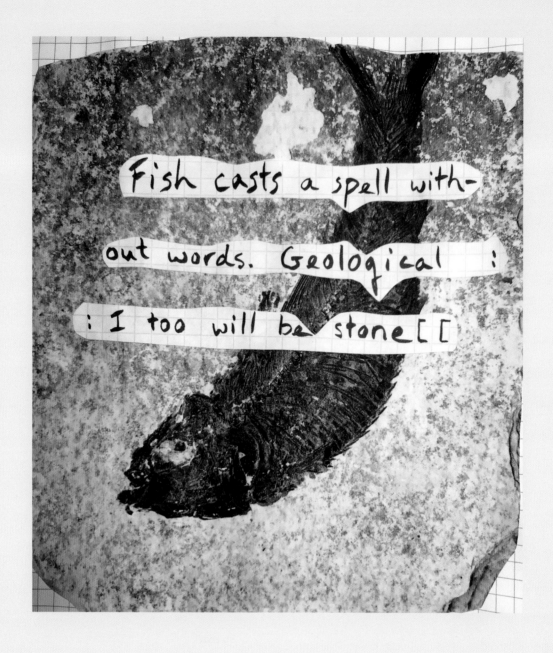

FIGURE 1.4

,

1966. A snapshot. Low country. Mom with me on the back of her bicycle. We both seem lost in the flats. Knew nothing of *The Order of Things* published the same year.

[[same year ('66) as post-Watts assemblage]
[knew nothing of this]
]]

FIGURE 1.5

] [
I

    So much disorder, things large and small

(small thing)

Leiden. Kindergarten. Don't know why, but I laugh so hard I pee my pants (the Dutch don't laugh much, even the kids). Teacher whisks me into the kitchen next to the classroom, peels away soaking underclothes door wide open, bottom turned toward the sky & she's scrubbing my bare skin in a sink (steel glinting blade) &kids wide-eyed &now they know how to

laugh

and then there was Dad (still in Leiden) in a **straitjacket** _____ _____ ___ _____

_____

(thing not so small) _____ _____ _____

_____ _____ _____

straitjacket in my head your most faithful *revenant*

your most faithful comingback fragment

(things large)
all the turmoil of the late 1960s but
we were far away lost in the flats

FRAGMENTS COMINGBACK / 19

The Oresteia comingback once more, this time as
Klytaimestra who's trashing Kassandra:

Oh she's mad. Hearkens only to
her own mad mind.

,

] [

I scattered into the future (climate crisis)   Kassandra can see it

a fiction? *A Drowned World*?

                      abandoned department stores, water-logged hotels, London sinking now a steamy lagoon
                      crawling with iguanas, swallowed by a Paleozoic past?

                                          No! says Kassandra. That's a novel, storyline unbroken, an
                                          Anthropocene tale, not the Holocene fragments I'm seeing

,

In the low country photograph you're holding something. Some pages.

Nonfiction.
Documentary.
Broken.   We like nonfiction because we live in fictitious times.

                      You unfold them now
                      these holocene fragments

]

    [

       [

                                                    and Kassandra

                                with her language that breaks open
                                           like dada in the desert

                                              OTOTOI POPOI DA!

                                  For her way of turning is that of a
                                          newcaught animal's

Animal Behavior

an altered book

(Michelle
artist & muse & scattered
packrat friend,
gifting this
fragment of a
long ago *Time-Life* book series:
most precious substrate)

substrate, noun, an underlying substance or layer; the surface or material on or from which an organism lives, grows, or obtains its nourishment.

using watercolour, pencil, acrylics, oils,
or simply gluing and pasting,
there's a substrate for everything.

Time-Life enchantment in a Bellaire Street living room and the comingback thrall of altered books

FIGURE 1.6

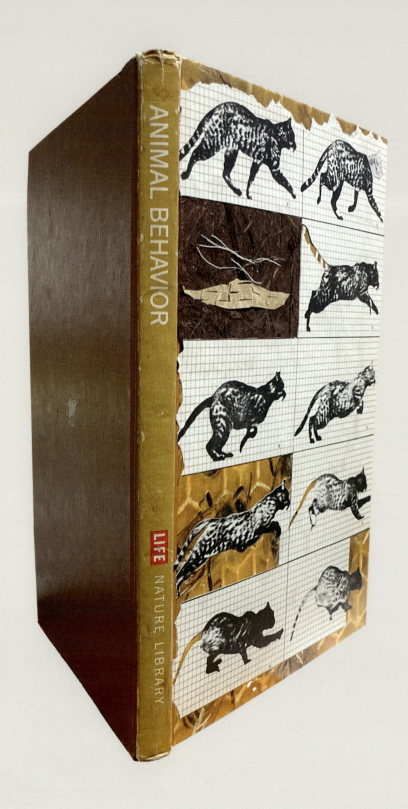

FIGURE 1.7

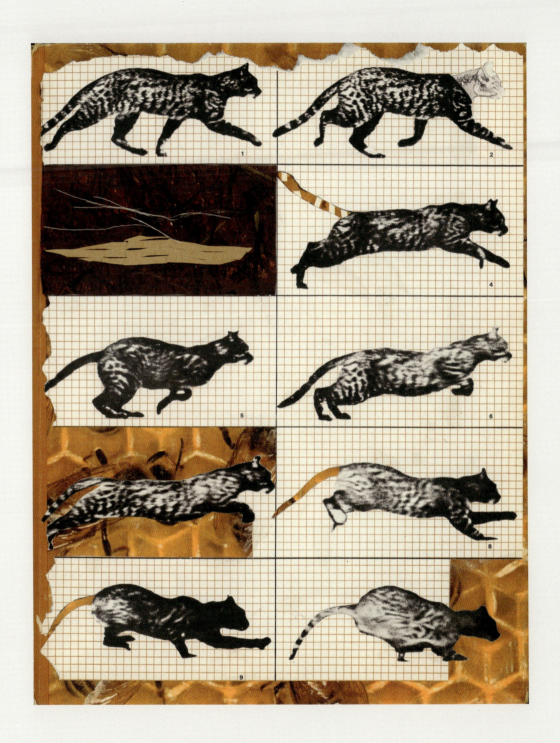

FIGURE 1.8

FIGURE 1.9

FIGURE 1.10

FIGURE 1.11

FIGURE 1.12

FIGURE 1.13

FIGURE 1.14

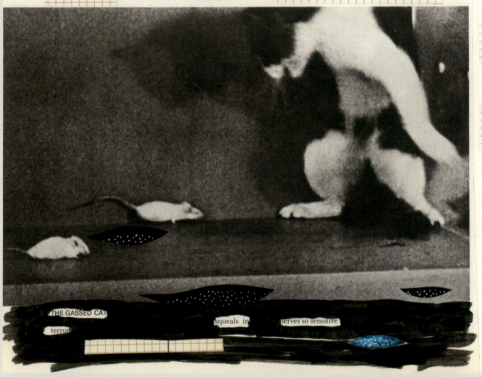

FIGURE 1.15

FIGURE 1.16

FIGURE 1.17

FIGURE 1.18

FIGURE 1.19

FIGURE 1.20

FIGURE 1.21

FIGURE 1.22

FIGURE 1.23

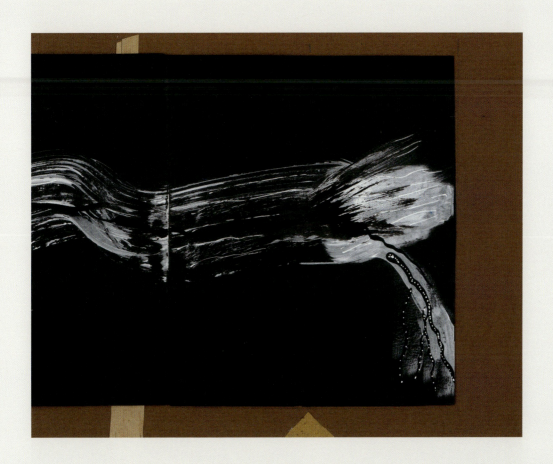

FIGURE 1.24

FIGURE 1.25

,

Kassandra's way of turning like a newcaught animal's. Turns to see the future. A prophet "sees it truly," but she's a foreigner (captive Trojan doesn't speak Greek), and "no one ever believes what she says." What's "ungraspable about Kassandra has to stay that way."

Futures set in motion with verbs. How silk "shimmers, billows, squints, spins, tucks, measures, pinches." Futures set in motion with "sliding": a book's energy derived from juxtaposed scenes, an *agencement* of fragments. *Vanitas*. Skull nesting in brown leaves with lavender fungi. Reading is sliding, although some don't slide. Can't slide, don't want to. Some stumble in the overburden of fragments. Some slip at the line break, suddenly narcoleptic. Drop plummet plunge sink dip buckle collapse: knees' abrupt cataplexy into the bone blank white of the page.

,

Another rule for writing:
la patte du peintre (literally, painter's paw):
let random constraint drive the dadabeat of your own unique fingers (or claws)

The ABCs of the Segmented Essay

Write the entire alphabet on a sheet of paper, then pick one letter. Make a list of all the things you can think of that start with that letter. (They need not be actual things, but can be ideas, concepts, emotions, etc.) Next choose one of the words from that list and write a brief paragraph about it. The next step is simply to repeat the previous steps: choose another letter, make a list of words that begin with that letter, select one word from the list, then write a brief paragraph about it. (You may repeat this process as many times as you wish.) Bingo: a segmented essay by juxtaposition is born.

A B C D E F G H I J K L M N O P Q R S T U V W X Y Z

lily love lemons lovely lively (lilypad) Lorenzo

    L is for lilypad. Lots of lilypads in the backyard pond on Adams Street. On a sunny afternoon you were sure to find a frog perched on a slick green platter. If frog was lucky, it would slip into the water as the blue heron's shadow crossed overhead, then shot down. Eventually beak met flesh. The frog population grew despite the culling by herons. This was due not only to the reproductive prowess of frogs, but also to the fact that the neighbor boy often brought frogs that had been stranded in the chlorine of their backyard pool.

A B C D E F G H I J K L M N O P Q R S T U V W X Y Z

(tiger) talented titillating tiny timid Tyrannosaurus

    T is for tiger. My friend Nayanika writes about tigers, not just paper ones, but flesh and blood beasts with teeth and claws, fur the color of cracked orange clay. She has lived among them in northern India, on the border with Tibet and Nepal. She has felt herself watched as she walked to the store, narrowly escaping becoming prey in a beastly tale. "Becoming Prey" is a famous title by Val Plumwood, feminist philosopher of nature, deathrolled by a crocodile in the East Alligator River in Kakadu National Park not once! not twice! but three times! Thricesurviving the deathroll. Not taken. (In Australian news reports about crocodile attacks a reporter will often write, "she was taken"). So too with Plumwood, twenty years after Kakadu:

            shewastaken

                      downdown taken

                                by a stroke

From the moment of birth, we're in a deathroll. To live is to enter the time of the will have been. Will be taken. Taken with a stroke, last mark of a pen. Finitude is ~~being~~ being taken. It will ~~be~~ you. "This breath could be your last." Such a sentence feels trite, like crocodile tears. You hear a meditating monk say the sentence during death meditation, but do you really believe it?

"T is for tiger." A slice of animal terror. How finitude *feels*.

These serpents slay men and they eat them weeping.

,

Renée Green's "Survival" exhales the new thought of a "canceling-out effect" of toomuchness. "In the midst of densities of information," there are "absences, lacunae, holes."

Holocene fragments can pause in the break of "that which is beyond understanding," comingback bits in the midst of coal mine disturbance,

in the midst of emptiness,
in the midst of glut,
where knowing too much we pass something over,

suffocated by a surfeit of things to be known.

Collaging born in restlessness, becoming respite: Holocene fragments
        in the midst of abandoned Anthropocene pits.

Collaging an exercise in constraint, like haiku (even the rule-breaking kind) for bearing the *unbearable*. Endurance of fragments.

bear, verb, old English *beran*,
to carry, bring; bring forth,
endure

You piece things together, sticky with glue, rearranging bits of broken-off world in order to

                in order to

                       How to finish this sentence?

(A meditation teacher tells you to beware of the "in order to" mind.

> IF YOU'RE LYING DOWN ROLL OVER ON YOUR SIDE BEFORE GETTING UP SO YOU DON'T LOSE YOUR BALANCE. SLIGHT LOSS OF BALANCE TODAY WHEN I TRIED BEING FRIENDLY

                       ,

Animals think-feel their way along a path.

For Hannah Arendt, "thinking resembles tracking, a kind of place 'beaten by the activity of thought,' which turns to ploddingly follow a course towards a pause." Fragments track the tracking, track the pause. (Pause gapping, willing nilling: décollage)

Pausing at ethics.

                       (Finger-wagging moralists incite rage.)

& Nietzsche wrote: "I deny morality as I deny alchemy. That is, I deny their presuppositions."

Don't deny! (double negative of the broken rule: not not saying Anthropocene)

Unsay

                    or listen for Kassandra's scream or for   windswept

OTOTOI POPOI DA!

dadainthedesert

Genealogy whispers through the archives: its speech is "gray, meticulous, and patiently documentary." Ethics begins with a suspicion of ethics. A suspicion of presuppositions. The ethical substrate. Something whispers, barely audible, just below its cracked surface. In the bloodied pits beneath morality's cover story.

we admire a text because 'it scatters well'

Futures set in motion as verbs.

Verbs that gather like deer among

fragments.

Verbs that say less and do more.

Less is more in the crumbling overburden

of morality's

cover story.

Apophatic:

Infinite regress of ethics talk.

Infinite regress of ethics talk

defined as talk about ethics.

Infinite regress of ethics talk

defined as talk about ethics

as ethics talk.

Infinite regress of ethics talk

defined as talk about ethics

talk's failure to define ethics as

something other

than just talk about ethics

ad infinitum

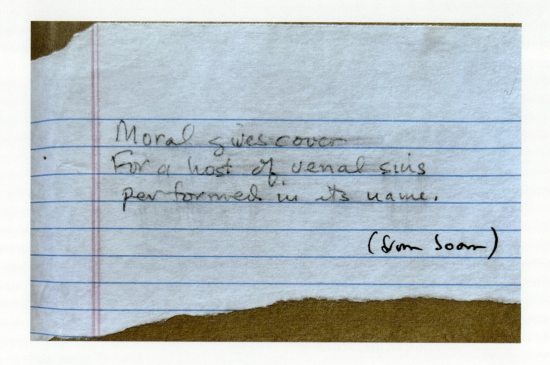

FIGURE 1.26

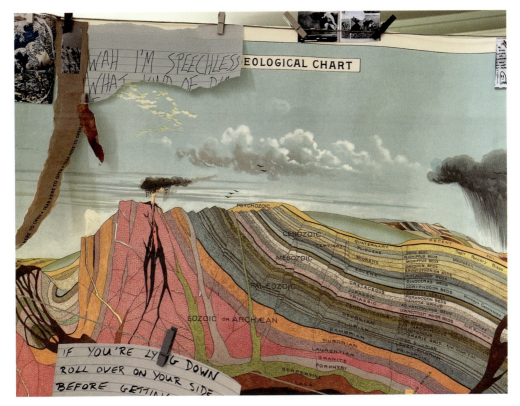

FIGURE 1.27

,

To collage is to track-think-feel this scattered ethics. Ethics is a verb: to track-think-feel fragments in archives. Family photos in a long-forgotten suitcase under a bed. Let their glow change you. A famous philosopher's love letters tucked away in a loose-leaf binder in someone's apartment. Asylum registers. Flyers from Black Panther rallies in Rose Library (in the same neighborhood where *Driving Miss Daisy* was filmed). Accounting books that track and measure the enslaved, the colonized, the queer. Cuvier's specimens.

> collage's parts always seem to be competing for a place

FRAGMENTS COMINGBACK / 47

in some unfinished
scene

who gives a shit?

,

Who gives a shit comes
hissing from behind a shard:
your polished fragment

so full of her own
endurance when the whole world
is crumbling. Stonecold.

[

[inhale] Start again.
In the grass dropped limbs re-cord
the bounce of childhood:

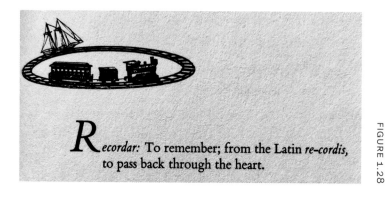

[exhale]

,

A B C D E F G H I J K L M N O P Q R S T U V W X Y Z

    O is for onion. In church basements everywhere, you hear that recovery's like an onion. Just keep peeling. One day at a time. 30 days, 90 days, a year. Decades of sobriety unpeeling. No core. The harder you look for yourself, the more I escapes you (let the I scatter).

A B C D E F G H I J K L M N O P Q R S T U V W X Y Z

    C is for chamomile. You never really liked chamomile tea. It's supposed to be soothing and god knows you need to be soothed. You bring the cup to your lips. You remember the honey smell. How you would crouch down at the edge of the dirt road that wound up Sunshine Canyon along cliff edges past the Gold Hill Inn to what is now Colorado Mountain Ranch but used to be the place where you married Dave on the side of a mountain and before that taught survival skills to kids at summer camp. Survival? They listened, wide-eyed.

    "You can last three days or more without any food. But only one without water. The most important thing is water."

    That smell! Greenyellow whiffs of summer. When you sip now. No smell. No flavor. You used to get angry at this absence in your cup. But you've learned to breathe. Emptiness becomes spacious. Breath instead of drink to calm you (Step 11).

FIGURE 1.29

FIGURE 1.30

,

neck craned

dream

mind teasing prayer flags

remnants flapping
remnants flapping
remnants flapping
remnants flapping

snake fang

not afraid

retreat slithers like

retreat slithers like
retreat slithers like
retreat slithers like
retreat slithers like
retreat slithers like
retreat slithers like
retreat slithers like
retreat slithers like

marks on a page

fleshy

,

              When the snake fang sinks
              into fleshy fingertip
              you are not afraid.

      How can this be? It's
      a dream. Retreat slithers off,
      writing slinks away.

      Fresh ink. Another
      fragment. For you, these new tracks
      in supplication:

heart cranked up, neck craned,
these thought remnants flapping like
mind teasing prayer flags.

How can this be?

neck craned

fingertip

cranked up

FIGURE 1.31

,

(thricerolled 5/7/5)

archives in fragments:
booklice feed on paper mold,
holes left behind by

silverfish scraping
their tiny sharp mandibles
over pocked faces

& moisture seeps &
ink bleeds & spine comes undone
& we become dust.

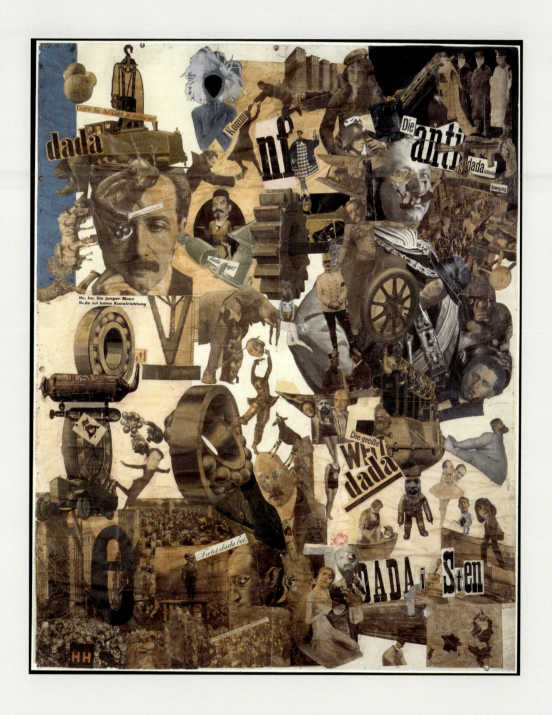

FIGURE 1.32 Hannah Höch, *Cut with the Kitchen Knife Dada through the Last Weimar Beer-Belly Cultural Epoch in Germany*, photomontage, 1919

,

"Knowledge . . . is made for cutting."
Borrowing Hannah Höch's kitchen knife: perfect sapphic collagist's tool. Before splicing and gluing comes cutting. Domestic. Re-calling (*re-cordis*) the dark of a Paris theater, first time seeing *Jeanne Dielman, 23 quai du Commerce, 1080 Bruxelles*, falling in love at the end, with the end, with this caesura in domestic order after being stuck in real time (unbearable, willthiseverend, 3 hours of repetitive tasks: peeling potatoes, setting the table, shining shoes, putting them on a shelf, pushing back a chair with a swing of the hip, breading veal, buttoning a shirt). Always the same peel set shine put push bread button peel set shine put push bread button peel set shine put push bread button set bread button bread button and then suddenly the cut

]

(décollage)

not the knife but its anticipation, an inner

] abyss gapes open

when Jeanne misses a button

and the audience

gasps [

,

Ubu Trump, the Vile Sovereign

My blade mimics hers,

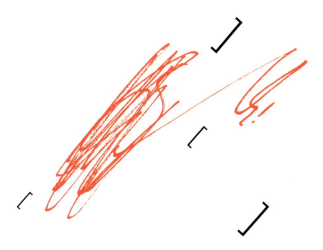

stabbing the wordvomiting belly

making it red like *Jeanne Dielman*

                                            the violence of paint
                        an attempt to remake the violence of reality itself

(can stabbing it here make it a small thing?)
                                                  "movedonherlikeabitch"

OTOTOI POPOI DA!

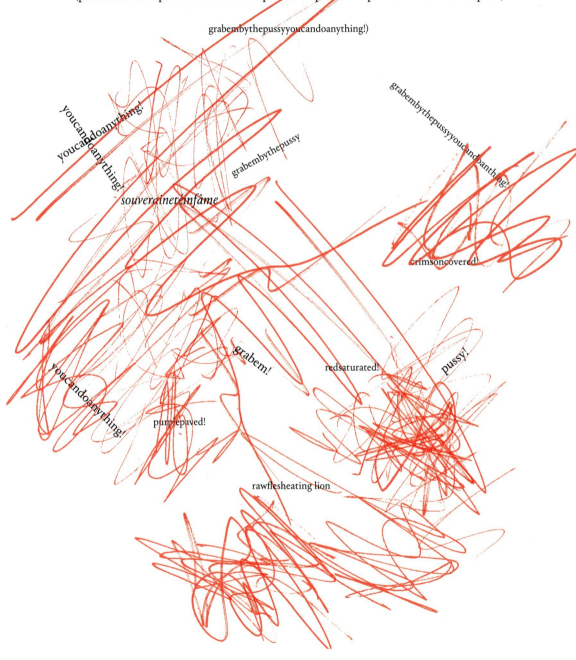

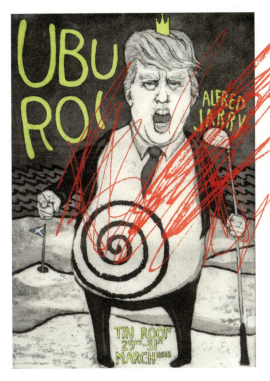

Père Ubu seizes power on a whim.
a toilet brush his scepter,
taking out the king, nobles,
finance ministers &
much of the population.
HIS SHIT SPREADS FAR AND WIDE

"administrative grotesque" of
clowns &
buffoons,
Mussolinis & Hitlers

grabembythepussy!

FIGURE 1.33

FIGURE 1.34

FRAGMENTS COMINGBACK / 61

FIGURE 1.35

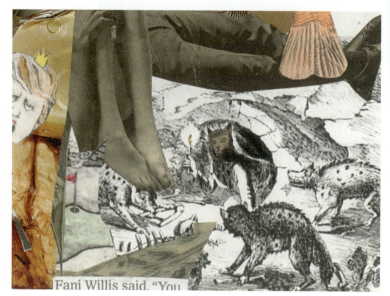

FIGURE 1.36

[inhale] Stab. Ubu Trump. ~~grabembythepussyyoucandoanything~~! Chop chop. The decapitated head with the tiny crown lands in a half-opened can of sardines. ~~grabem!~~ Snip snip. A rotten onion settles into the space above Ubu's paunch. Hand raised, brandishing a golf club or maybe a toilet brush? ~~grabembythepussy!~~ Chop chop. Blood spatter drips. A dart hits the bull's-eye of Ubu's belly. Fish swarm the chaos of darts, rotting fruit, a vortex of hundred-dollar bills. More blood spatter blots out Ben Franklin's face. A cat in the mouth of the Kirkdale Cave fends off a mob of hyenas standing guard over Ubu's putting green. Onion skin everywhere unpeeling. Up toward the surface comes Kevin Beasley's sculpture *Strange Fruit*. Beasley's ~~lynched~~ bodies drop toward banana skins. Above, yahoos in MAGA hats grope the Capitol walls, monkeys. At the center, Fani Willis scrapes things back (onion-peel queen, can we call her brave?). Cheering from the sidelines a bad-ass mermaid nurse with water wings.

FIGURE 1.37

"An investigation is like an onion. You never know. You pull something back, and then you find something else."

murdering the text, literally
cutting it into pieces

OTOTOI POPOI DA!

,

On January 6th the mob comes, blinding white. Some move in tight formation in tactical gear. Others come bearing flagpoles, zip ties, bear spray, crutches. Everything becomes a weapon. "A defiance of authority," scorching rage. The crowd burns. A retired firefighter throws a fire extinguisher at Capitol police, cracks open Brian Sicknick's skull, fatal. Someone parades a Confederate flag across the antique mosaic floor, someone else wears a Camp Auschwitz shirt. "Outside, makeshift gallows [stand], complete with sturdy wooden steps and the noose."

Robert Sanford
Kevin Seefried
Robert Keith Packer

All night long]   I am aware

             ] of evildoing

To *break* into tears seems the right verb

,

shattered and scattered

,

into the nation
of
cry
into language that breaks open
like dada in the desert these comingback fragments of a body politic not whole never was just nation imagination for

FIGURE 1.38

some [for many not nation neverwas [[

,

    My childhood friend says the world is changing for the better.
    "Look at all the women getting elected," she says. "Women are different. More peaceful."
    AOC hid in Katie Porter's office, terrified, lights out, no talking. She borrowed a staffer's athletic shoes in case she had to run. Ubu's mob would have killed her if they'd found her. The mob was cheered on by another woman elected by Georgians, sisterhood forever. Addwomenandstir feminism. Equality means women can now hunt like men. Marjorie Taylor Greene is on the hunt: scanning the heavens for Jews with laser beams, or prowling the underbrush for Satanists, pedophiles, and lizard people.
    "Many members of Congress are afraid to be in the building with her."
    ~~Moveonherlikeabitch.~~ Chop chop, snip snip, jab jab. A tear here, a cut there, I light a match to edge the paper with bright flame. Poof. Poof. Fire goes out, dark ash floats in the air. This counter-chopping-and-scorching feels like respite.
    I dab glue over burnt shapes. Gently, with great care, I pretend to put the world back together again.

FIGURE 1.39

,

Beautiful thing! aflame   .

                                    a defiance of authority

   —burnt Sappho's poems, burned

   (by intention or are they still hid

   in the Vatican crypts?)   :

                            beauty is

a defiance of authority   :

                      for they were

unwrapped, fragment by fragment, from

outer mummy cases of papier-mâché, inside

Egyptian sarcophagi

FIGURE 1.40

,

[You for] the fragrant-bosomed [Muses'] lovely gifts
[be zealous,] girls, [and the] clear melodious lyre:

[but my once tender] body old age now
[has seized:] my hair's turned [white] instead of dark

,

]

there is a space where a thought would be, but which you can't get hold of.
I love that space.

[if you're singing or talking take a breath]

,

] the fragrant-bosomed   lovely gifts
] girls,   clear melodious lyre:

] body old age now
] my hair's turned   instead of dark

,

Sappho : Plato :: fragment : whole
fragment : whole :: particular : general

analogy is an inference or an argument from one particular to another particular, as opposed to deduction, induction, and abduction, in which at least one of the premises, or the conclusion, is general rather than particular in nature.

,

particularities endure while generalities crumble

[so much for metaphysics]

aplacewhereathoughtshouldbe
lovethatspace

FIGURE 1.41

,

    Oh that I had wings like a dove! For then
would I fly away, and be at rest.

,

    What is God's will for a wing?
Every bird knows that.

,

Ask the sub sub librarian, bits of paper tacked to the wall with blue painter's tape.
Ask the cutout
fragments hanging from laundry lines across my living space. Ask the glued pages of a

FRAGMENTS COMINGBACK / 71

blackbacked sketchbook. Ask the basket of ribbons, confetti, jute, black ink, crinkled leaves, dried daisies, sepia photos, white fur from the IAS woods ("something died here," Wendy said). My archive.

I, scattered,

                my archiv

Ask her for images and patterns. Find a scrap. A double-sided picture with handwritten words. Place it in my looking-glass hands.

FIGURE 1.42

,

The bird wing envelops the girl. In the white margin a whisper in faded pencil:

I love you so much.
lovethatspace

On the flip side of the image is another pairing: you and me, again. You, Michelle the

markmaking muse and bringer of substrate, me, blond, both of us scattered back into Denver livingroom.

72 / THESE SURVIVALS

FIGURE 1.43

We huddle in front of a window. *Time-Life* substrate held open across our laps. I read, bossy teacher. You look on. I encircle the white pages, a fist here, a palm there. You all angles, trying to get in, body wedged sideways, face anxious peering down, fingers curved (*la patte du peintre*) over bluesloped sleeve.

Years pass. Pages turn. No holding them back.
You've lost so much. *Dis-aster*.

,

Disaster, n.
Anything that befalls of ruinous or distressing nature; any unfortunate event, especially a sudden or great misfortune, 1590s, from Middle French *désastre* (1560s), from Italian *disastro*, literally "ill-starred," from *dis-*, here merely pejorative, equivalent to English *mis-* "ill" (see dis-) + *astro* "star, planet," from Latin *astrum*, from Greek *astron* "star."

,

You called me in Houston in the middle of the night: "Help, Bunny, he's going to die." Your brother, Vincent, ill-starred one night on a patch of ice, fast car turned lethal in a Wyoming blizzard between Laramie and Cheyenne. And then your father, stubborn to the last breath, still lighting up as he gasped for air, pulling back the oxygen mask, taking another puff. And then your mother, gulping down ibuprofen to ease the pain. She went for tests: all clear, the doctor said. A week later, a phone call: our mistake. Cancer feeding on her liver for years, it looks like Swiss cheese, the nurse said.

Michelle, now I'm looking over your shoulder. I hope you don't mind. Could you have gone on if you'd known what was coming?

,

Astrum sinistrum.
The sense is astrological, of a calamity blamed on an unfavorable position of a planet, and "star" here is probably meant in the astrological sense of "destiny, fortune, fate." Compare medieval Latin *astrum sinistrum* "misfortune," literally "unlucky star," and English "ill-starred."

,

I look down, again, at the book I'm writing: these survivals. In our sixties now, no blond no brunette, we are gray. Skeleton letters—I love you so much—whispering archive in graphite, the L and the V half gone, enduring.

"Genealogy is gray," exquisite, like your charcoal drawings taking flight.

Here's a joyful face in the tree bark, contracting and expanding like bird wings. Floosh

    p p p

        sound of a pigeon. Humble.

      Friends for half a century. This is what is, who we are together,

          what we are doing.

FIGURE 1.44

II

IN THE MIDDLE
IN THE DARK
BETWEEN US

]

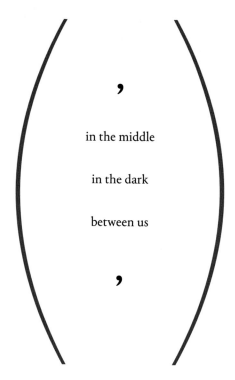

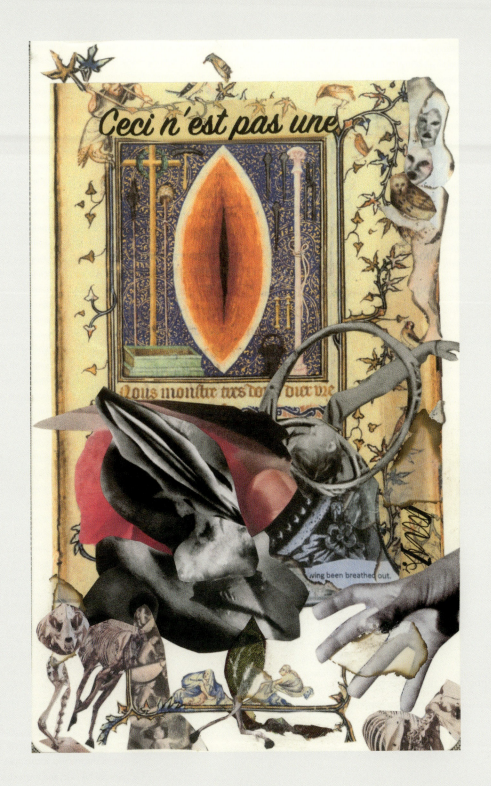

FIGURE 2.1

,

           the last time I heard you
                  you said
  ]
  ]
  ] I will go

Yet here you are again,
]   led   astray

,

           why again?

                                        comingback fragment
        trying to say something
          trying to unsay it

,

Just look, you say. Here I am again. With these fragments. For readings that slide.
I'm not what you think.
I'm not nothing.

                I'm God made flesh.
           Flesh opened as wound. Salvation.
       Surrounded here by the torturer's tools (*arma Christi*),
      sure signs of that sacred savaging of a body savaging
    that will save you and you and you (you not everyone of course not

those we call savages heathens heretics)
passion on the cross, expiring for us, and then

                                      one of the soldiers with a spear
                                      pierced his side, and forthwith
                                      came there out blood and water

FIGURE 2.2

,

Isolated for contemplation. At least 3 *pattes des peintre*s (pawprints in clay) in this *grisaille* and gold leaf miniature: Jean le Noir, his daughter Bourgot, and his workshop. The end of Bonne de Luxembourg's story is a wound. A mysterical substrate (collaging's sapphic ground)

$$\left(\begin{array}{ll} \text{filling the} & \text{composition} \\ \text{a gaping, dis} & \text{embodied wound} \\ \text{almond-sh} & \text{aped ring} \\ \text{orange} & \text{-red} \\ \text{torn} & \text{flesh} \\ \text{ver} & \text{tical} \\ \text{brown gash} & \text{in the center} \\ \text{actual size} & \text{(about 2 inches)} \end{array} \right)$$

(a small thing)

,

Keep looking, you say. I know you could gaze at this

crimsoncovered

redsaturated

fleshforever

(And really, isn't it true that the most erotic place *onthebody* is **là**   *où le vêtement baille?*
 []
 ~~there~~ where the garment gapes?

It's intermittence   that's erotic   :   flesh that scintillates *between two*

pieces; it's the scintillation itself that seduces   or encore   :

the mise-en-scène of

appearance   /   disappearance.)

Turn back the pages: another miniature, second to last (folio 328r: *The Crucifixion*)

84 / THESE SURVIVALS

ill luminations

in psalters:
lookjustlook!
woundedness pointing:
pointing back at itself!
(but everyone knows the
wound is postmortem:
how can it point if the
pointer is dead?)
pointing back comingback
postmortem fragment
mise-en-scène of
appearance/disappearance
wound fragment
just below the curve of the
right breast
(small-breasted fragment)
body angular, pale,
nice and slim, European
looking
a pair of angels thin as
wallpaper piloting behind
the body where the
garment gapes (*là où le
vêtement baille*)
another pair kneeling
like angels landing:
Bonne
(*bonne*, feminine of *bon*
we all know means good),
with her husband
the future French king,
John the Good, so good!

(but really, these two?
Nietzsche's
blond beasts,
no doubt about it)

FIGURE 2.3

] the cut of a spear covers over
the cut
of dissectingknives sculpting
grabembythepussyyoucandoanything
parts in centerfoldsandjars:
Manmuseum full of shelves, endless pages,
wordvomiting prayerbooks for manminded gynecological
crimsoncovered planet
almost every corner blondbeasted

IN THE MIDDLE, IN THE DARK / 85

                                                                                               how to unsay this
                                                                                            how to break the jar?

!

,

In this afterGod secular world, I remade you. I remade you, collaging directly into the wound.

(Gasp in a dark theater).

                                                                                In search of transcendence?
                                                                       Or utterly inside this immanence?

                      So inside the wound I became you?
                      Twenty-first-century mystic

                                        (mystic hystericized, *la mystérique*
                                        c'est moi, straitjacket in my head)

                                        Oh she's mad. Hearkens only to
                                        her own mad mind.

no longer looking up
              heart dialed down
                          neck bent down
                                        downdown
                                          downtakendowntakendown

                        takendown into something like a
                                        GodunsayingGod

I cut you with a kitchen knife, glued you to white paper, the very last page in my own

clothbound psalter. Godunsaying for holding stayingwith beingwith breathingwithyou

                          in the middle
                          in the dark
                          between us

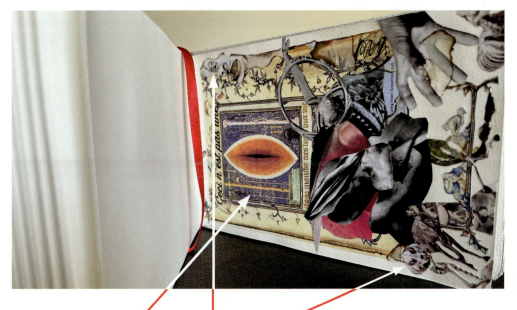

FIGURE 2.4

inthemiddleinthedarkbetweenusinthemiddleinthedarkbetweenusinthemiddleinthedarkbetweenus

an illuminated prayer book					middle (ages)
Cuvier's skeletons						middle (earth)
Ellen Gallagher's rendering of Drexciya (*Watery Ecstatic*)	middle (passage)

,

Cutting and pasting: it was in making you that this rage (*Jeanne Dielman*'s missed buttonhole)

became (for a moment) something else: act of devotion:

                        hardcover substrate, the book into which I inserted you
        unfolded like a   prayer book, dug up and
          [ ]   opened,   you unwrapped
        [yourself] fragment by fragment, from
               outer mummy cases of papier-mâché and
     our dadabeat together felt   likerocking
        between the covers and you calmed me   likethedesert

IN THE MIDDLE, IN THE DARK

calmed covid calmed capitol calmed chaos calmed crazy calmed

comingback fragment straitjacket in my head

then (more cutting) this sapphic fragment (used and reused how many times?)

FIGURE 2.5

collaging proliferation, copies of copies, some sapphic bot

> **Sappho Bot** @sapphobot · Aug 27, 2021
> Sweet mother, I cannot weave –
> slender Aphrodite has overcome me
> with longing for a girl.
> 💬 4   🔁 253   ♡ 1.6K

FIGURE 2.6

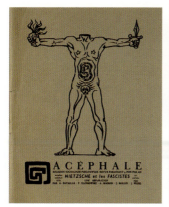 

FIGURES 2.7 and 2.8

decapitated   (you may think this cruel but)   sacred conjuration

this beheading like "the violence of paint.... We nearly always live through screens—a screened existence. And I sometimes think, when people say my work is violent, that I have been able to clear away one or two of the veils or screens."

and it's true

"human life is exasperated by having served as the head and reason of the universe

         and it's necessary

                to become different

                                                                        [[sapphic]]

             "the best day of my life—
                 my rebirthday,
                 so to speak—   or cease to be"
     and   was when I found I had no head"

you teach me something

like practicing love's persistence in the midst of *dés-astre*

                                           unsaying (a-lethia) in fragments

<small>comingback fragment this maternal finitude thiswah I'm speechless this sapphic abysscomingback fragment this maternal finitude thiswah I'm speechless this sapphic abyss comingback fragment this maternal finitude thiswah I'm speechless this sapphic abyss comingback fragment this maternal finitude thiswah I'm speechless this sapphic abyss comingback fragment this maternalfinitude thiswah I'm speechless this sapphic abyss comingback fragment this maternal finitude thiswah I'm speechless this sapphic abyssthis</small>

comingback fragment this maternal finitude thiswah I'm speechless this sapphic abysscomingback fragment this maternal finitude

IN THE MIDDLE, IN THE DARK / 89

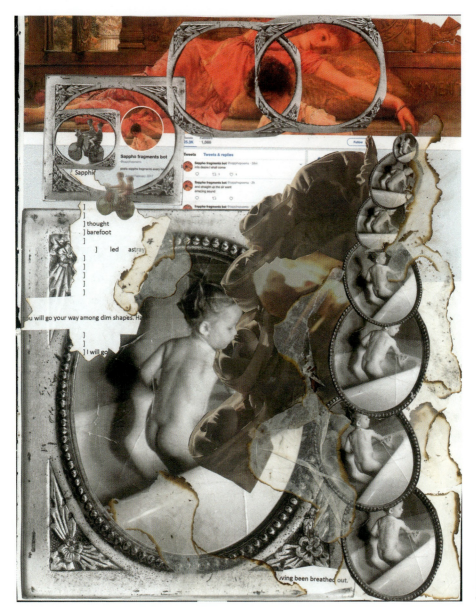

FIGURE 2.9

comingback fragment this maternal finitude thiswah I'm speechless this sapphic abysscomingback fragment this maternal finitude thiswah I'm speechless this sapphic abyss

comingback fragment this maternal finitude thiswah I'm speechless this sapphic abyss comingback fragment this maternal finitude thiswah I'm speechless this sapphic abyss

comingback fragment this maternalfinitude thiswah I'm speechless this sapphic abyss comingback fragment this maternal finitude thiswah I'm speechless this sapphic abyssthis

comingback fragment this maternal finitude thiswah I'm speechless this sapphic abysscomingback fragment this maternal finitude thiswah I'm speechless this sapphic abyss comingback fragment this maternal finitude thiswah I'm speechless this sapphic abyss

this abyss
apophatic
sapphobot

90 / THESE SURVIVALS

,

I made you during covid and the first reign of DonaldtheBad. Now you're back. Looking at you again on the internet, cloistersdotcom. Going and meeting you in person at the Cloisters, on a hill above the Hudson on a code red smoke day, gallery 13, Bonne de Luxembourg's Prayer Book under glass. Opened to the wrong page. I couldn't see you but I knew you were there. Eyeswatering throatburning in a medieval garden clogged with toxic air from outofcontrol wildfires in Quebec. Will you still be here, preserved in a case, in another 500 years?

Back in Princeton, closing the windows, turning on the HEPA filter, printing you out again again again Cutting you up again, gluing you back together again. Hanging you from clotheslines. Again. Making you my own again:

        sapphic

        in all the ways (historical) you can imagine

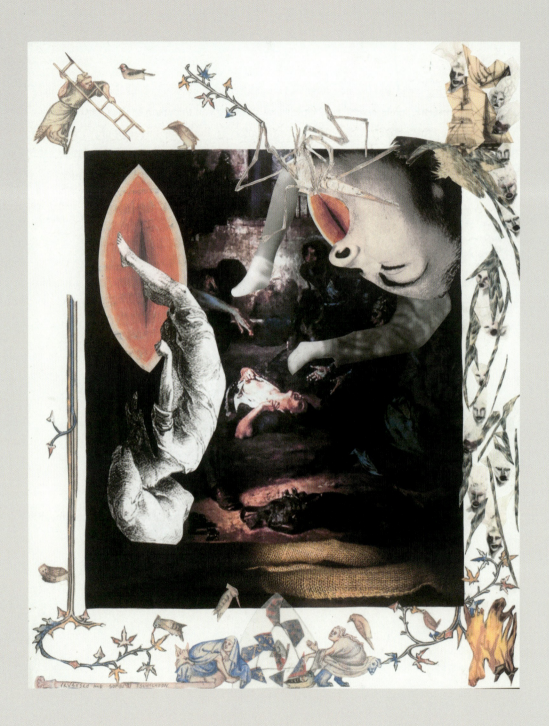

FIGURE 2.10

: *mystérique*

    mystichystericmystichystericmystichysteric

        what I loved in you most still do are these treacherous transformations

            treachery of images *ceci n'est pas une pipe*

                selfunsaying speech

                    your mute backtalking brilliant selfunraveling

                                      like Kassandra

                in the middle

                            as a difference you cannot grasp

                    a glass that does not give back the image placed before it

What you un/said to the blond beasts (greedy sovereigns, grabby Trumps, &cold Cuviers):

I'm not what you think, you said, unsaying:

I'm not what you think you can know by seeing (because there it is, anyone can see it,

        we all know pornography [comparative anatomy] when we see it)

                                          grabembythepussy
                                              putitinajar

I'm not what you think you can know by seeing because what you're seeing is your own not-seeing,

                                                      (pornotroping)

not-seeing your own seeing as pornographic overseeing

not-seeing pornographic overseeing as pornographic overknowing that cannot see or know not only what it sees but especially its own not-seeing

                (history of science, history of art:

                          knowing it too much, you pass something over)

but you think you know because all you see is your own not-seeing not-knowing:

                                                moveonherlikeabitch

overknowing that knows nothing, overseeing that sees nothing

  because

        to you   (still life vanitas)

I am nothing but nothingness (like coal mine overburden),

                      un rien-à-voir,

                            a

                    nothing-to-see.

,

How to escape this infinite regress, algorithmic botting blotting us out

(How can I say it? How can I unsay it?)

    to say I'm not nothing leads to infinite regress

                                                         jar breaks, pussy bolts:
                                                         I'm not nothing!

to say I'm not nothing (double negation)   I'm not a ~~split beaver~~ not a
                                                squeezeboxvaginavagcuntbeaverpounani
                                                grabembythepussyyoucandoanything
                                                  not an abject comingback fragment

requires saying/unsaying: I am/I am not

                                      ad infinitum

                                                      I'm/not I'm/not I'm/not I'm/not I'm/not

FIGURE 2.11

FIGURE 2.12

(refusing to interpret you)　　　just sing　　　　　for yourself

andnooneelse

foryourselfandnooneelse foryourselfandnooneelse foryourselfandnooneelse foryourselfandnooneelse

foryourselfandnooneelse

,

Nothing starts or ends with birth. (In the beginning there's disparity.)
Birth breaks a path, a path toward death, path that we slide:
we thinking-tracking along births and deaths. Birth births death, death deaths birth.
Unbearable myowndeaththought (like all belovedsdying)

but moreso thissapphicmotherdeath, this 6th xtinction means end of the line (species caesura):
end of the path that slides & breaks.

X no more deaths birthed
  no more births deathed
  = birth breached
  = death deathed

in Delhi the vultures are gone & now kites soar like flying lizards &on redzone days they plummet from the sky like meteors

Motherdying (sapphic fragment) uncovering the place you came from,
 alēthēs (not concealing):

  pause gapping willing nilling missed buttonhole

 gasping in a dark theater, another we

  tumbling down

   into a fissure in a planet

  sixthextinction worlds ending &ending (alreadyended)
   we inthemiddleof &anotherending

breach, verb, to make a gap (planetary boundaries
breached)

 will a we griefremembering bone, mummy, ash, soil

   begin again?

Entering the dark slit means being with this we vultures&kites&all
  mannerofbeastsamongus

 havingbeenwillbetaken

 [time of unreason]

 wings flying fluttering
 spatter of plosives
 final open
 vowel's escape

 ἐκπεποταμένα

,

When I made you my devotional, homebodied and terrified, did I register this mimicry of a

medieval queen? Bonne dying not of covid but an earlier plague? Euroqueenmother with all her

whitegirl privilege but still the reaper lurks presenting ruptures like bubos

[poised over the abyss of the]
willbetaken
[and the]
havingbeen

(The plague hits Western Europe in 1347, impervious to rank, wealth, age.
By 1350 nearly a third of the population suddenly willbetaken.)

1349. Maubuisson, France. Thirty-four years old. Motherdying. Did her part to keep the bluebloodline going. Ten deliveries in ten years. Her firstborn, Charles, will be king, succeeding his father, John the Good. Every labor agony. Each contraction a stab in the dark. In the unbearable, opening her psalter, final page drawing her into redlipped darkness.

Blood and pus seeping from bubopocked groin, neck, armpits. Vomit rising to her throat. Dry heaves. Nothing left to expel. Body shivering, sweating. Hours of this. Night falls. At last. Last exhale bringing respite. Ekpepotamena.

Bluebloodlinebluebloodlinebluebloodlinebluebloodlinebluebloodlinebluebloodlinebluebloodlinebluebloodlineblueb

$$\Bigg(\overset{\displaystyle,}{\underset{\displaystyle}{\begin{array}{c}\text{Eros is a verb:}\\ \text{caress, kiss, drink from, bathe in, enter}\\ \text{this}\\ \text{selfemptying darkness}\end{array}}}\Bigg)$$

loodbluebloodlinebluebloodlinebluebloodlinebluebloodlinebluebloodlinebluebloodlinebluebloodlinebluebloodlinebluebloodlinebl

Ecstasy is there in that glorious slit where she curls up in her nest, where she rests as if she had found her home.

,

and **perception** retreats or
rather

turns   turning like a newcaught animal

toward

this

dark

(vestibular)

interiority

that isn't my own

yet not outside me

le réseau carcéral n'a pas de dehors

no outside

no outside

no outside

just an
asymptotical tending

toward the limits of one's own life

unflinching

asymptotical curve spiraling up up upupup
like bubbles bubbling up like griefremembering
drexciya watery ecstasy on the upper right side
sliding down the righthand side this sliding a
tender tending a tender tending a tendertending
that tenderlytends toward griefremembering
tenderness

curve of tenderness

this griefremembering tending   hold cannot be told yet must
be told, but only through its untelling

inside this dark interiority that isn't my own

[ ] can I hold thisunholding [

what is black inside the museums of paris?
                        ungrasping ungrabbing
                                undisplay   unmanned
                                                                                 unmuseum
                                                                                   unsaying

suddenlywe

                                                                                        like Kassandra
                                                                                   in the middle
                                                                          (ages, earth, passage)
                                                   as a difference we cannot grasp
a glass that does not give back the image placed before it

III

DÉCOLLAGE

,

(prostration)
like a cat rubbing up against your leg

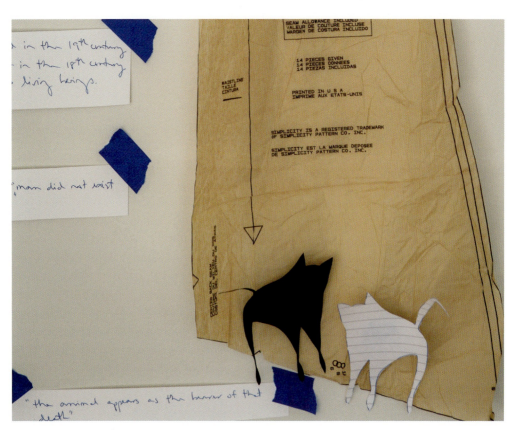

FIGURE 3.1

    making *Garments against Women* she learned
       the key to everything was not the
               time
              spent
    on the machine but the time spent
         with a ~~needle~~ in

              hand

                                                [~~needle~~ = scissors glue stick ink])

FIGURE 3.2

FIGURE 3.3

FIGURE 3.4

FIGURE 3.5

FIGURE 3.6

FIGURE 3.7

FIGURE 3.8

FIGURE 3.9

FIGURE 3.10

FIGURE 3.11

FIGURE 3.12

FIGURE 3.13

FIGURE 3.14

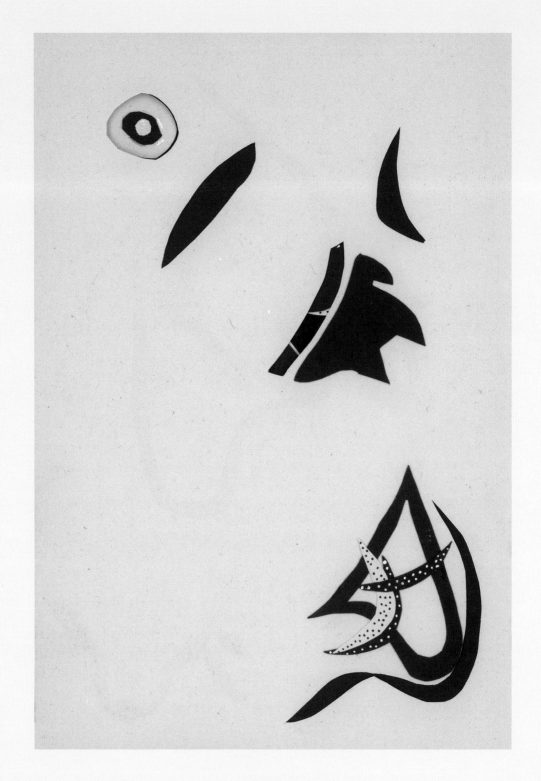

FIGURE 3.15

FIGURE 3.16

FIGURE 3.17

FIGURE 3.18

FIGURE 3.19

FIGURE 3.20

FIGURE 3.21

,

Fragments composed in multiple stages.

Rough copy, overcooked, thrownwet spaghetti at a wall
(start somewhere see what sticks)

: scribbles paper scraps painters tape patterns erasures numbers quotes rules poems proustian *paperoles* (so beautiful to look at no longer care what they say) (my own) assiduously composed scholarprose
hacked to pieces

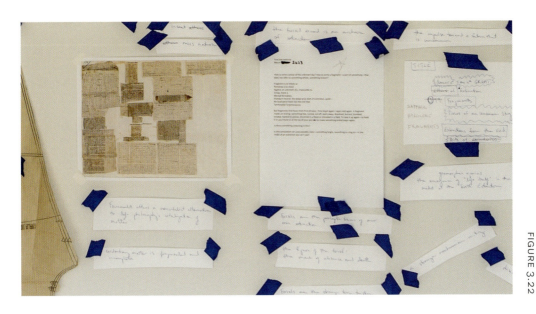

FIGURE 3.22

DÉCOLLAGE / 129

FIGURE 3.23

probably more meaningful to
sew a dress than to write a poem

And then one night a new constellation (first draft) zigzagged its way across my study

FIGURE 3.24

FIGURE 3.25

and then lines took over (second draft) crisscrossing the living room and then lower down (third draft) at the chest descended again (fourth) to hips and knees (tripline) and then behind me (fifth) spinning like a web.

FIGURE 3.26

FIGURE 3.27

Assiduous spider. Dragline silk, crossbeaming structures for images and letters. But strung up, paintertaped, or glued into a book with a choppedout spine (sixth and final) of these tattered

garments
feral fragilités

<h2 style="text-align:center">these collages beyond saving</h2>

less nouns &more verbs: prostrations and offerings, cat rubbing against your leg
thesebeloved

DÉCOLLAGE / 131

verbs enduring while nouns crumble

forms (nouns) do not matter in themselves

rub, v, early 14th c. *rubben* to apply friction to a surface like cat pheromones leaving their scent
(possession feels like love)

I know that smell

on dresspattern catcutout yellowonion skin tissue paper glue chanced upon in the kitchen embroidery thread butcher paper whiteinkblackinkgoldinksilverink fruit netting(white) fruit netting(red) *New Yorker* typeface maskingtape morepainterstape scotchtape artiststape weatherreport writing fancytapegiftedfromastudent corrugations ink magicmarkers newsprint (already yellowed) blue sheets of plastic *New York Times* headlines dirtdarkened string muskyfur rusted brillopad jute fibers seedpods sequins &glitter &spangles &stickers &decimatedbooks for altering

,

prostrations for survival

,

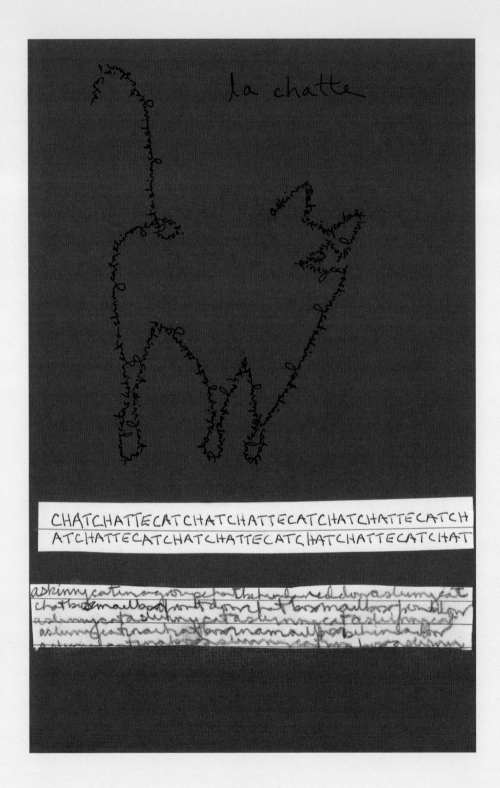

FIGURE 3.28

FIGURE 3.29

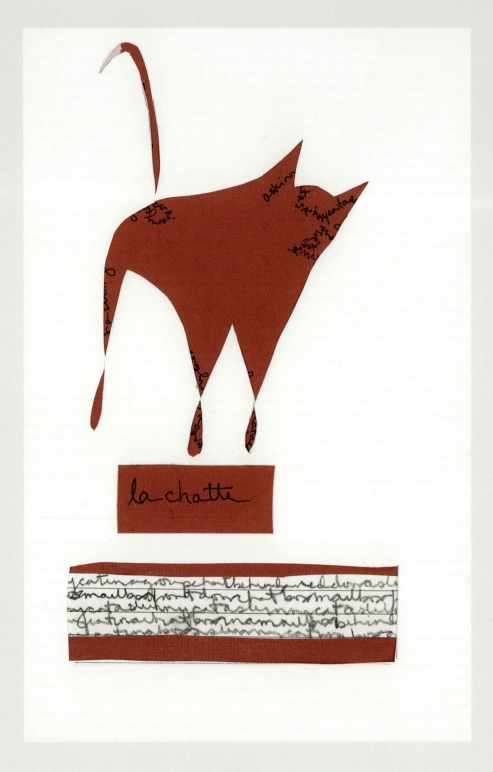

FIGURE 3.30

FIGURE 3.31

FIGURE 3.32

,

One day perhaps we will no longer know what this was. No archival box will preserve

this scent

these rubbings

weird anarchic portrait weird history of a present inadadajunkyard
weird sapphobotic speech weird mysterical prayer

to some secular GodnotGod

         higherpower met low
           downdown in
            AA basements
            (years&years)

       kites
         fall
           like
              fragments
         from the skies
             of Delhi
        in a basement they repair a wing

fragments may endure but the whole crumbles

inexorable

unhumaning holoscenic décollage

DÉCOLLAGE

FIGURE 3.33 Lorraine O'Grady, *Haiku Diptych 7*, from *Cutting Out CONYT* (1977/2017).

,

> **Weather Reports**
>
> [let constraint drive the beat of décollage]
>
> Go to David Lynch Weather Report and listen to some of his weather reports.
> Then set your timer for 5 minutes and write a weather report.
> Report on the weather sometime during the last 8 hours.
> Where were you?
> What were you thinking about?

Yesterday was sunny but surprisingly cold. I was next to the Princeton golf course and saw a young couple walking across the putting green as the wind blew their hair, golf balls flying. I was thinking huge risk. But understood the walking with all that energy in the air. Made a stray golf ball feel like nothingthatcouldkillyou. Air all smiles, daffodils & magnolias. Like today, sunny again high 50s. Spring on the way. You forgot about climate crisis. Will eat smoked fish for supper. How long does it take to play a game of golf?

,

Back in Atlanta. Another report. *Sur le vif*. Right now. This is not a drill. (Treachery of images: not a haiku or abc segmented essay or weather report or selftweeting bot)

3 pm but suddenly nightfalling dark. Windhowl hisses, leaves frantic. Tornado warnings throughout the South. On the I-screen red rings spreading, swallowing the blue dot where we live. Looking up from alarmbelling storm tracker app, beyond the windows to the trees. Frenzied. Gusts, apocalyptic. Brainalarm ringing, algorithmic, faster than the speed of consciousness. More thunderclaps. Impending disaster, any minute sudden death. Are we prepared for this? Is this the final earthquake volcano tornado plague hurricane fire

endoftheworld Big One? Do we have extra candles? Bottled water? Canned goods? Vision blurred by Sapphobot fearseeing snapshots of dayaftertomorrow when storms are done but kudzu chokes us wringing our necks & pythons slither up from the Everglades &serpents jaw opens to swallow ourhome &OMG another plague comes seeping let's close the windows stuff rags in the underdoor push back the creepycrawly worse than aids or covid or Bonnewithherbubos this stealth penetration will enter our lungs our pores every hole in our body we will die in agony mothermatter dyingwithus gasping for breath.

,

Planetary ill. So ill. Feverish. Seas rising. Airless cities wracked with coughing. Toxic overburden vomits fluid over skyscrapers & heaves sewage into subway tunnels rats scattering thisbreath sohot sohot feverbreath heating all that breathes in the alleys in the basements on rooftops in Delhi or New York or the mountains of Tibet or the valleys of its glaciers melting becoming ocean brooding monsterstorms hatching hurricanes liquifying poles &axis of rotation tilts fainting eastward into space can we feel it? Fever's rising again, this time higher. Lightning flashes. Ill lumination withoutGod. Fires burning. Convulsed planetweakening. Rash spreading (timelapse maps tracking) coast to coast skin inflaming redder&redder&redder&redder the whole earth bright redzone

,

Cut!

    Time for another fragment
                      sharp-bladed

                                                                    edge.
Décollaging algorithmic assemblage. Sapphobot not knowledge but incitement of
fear   can we call her brave?
            not knowledge not a story
                                                        murder the text, literally
                                                        cut it into pieces

remembering the past still with us

some things can't be told

                                                    Zong! is the Song of the untold
                                                    story; it cannot be told yet must
                                                    be told, but only through its untelling

        just cut, poetic

                    line breaks with kitchen knives (better tool than twittering sapphic bots)

                                    ,

Gaps gape like missed buttonholes. Nine planetary boundaries
                                                    like line breaks
                                            in earth   /   sea   /   sky//
                        (desert dadabeat drumming vestibular fields &domestic interiors)

                but where the lines break   in the break
                                        impossible to say:

                            ]
                            ]
                            deep sound
                            ]

sapphic fragments lack precision

                                            a single square bracket gives the impression of
                                            missing matter
                                            ] or [

these brackets cannot track
                every thinking-feeling griefremembering

every disappearance					a blizzard of marks

every emptying

    cannot be told yet must

        be told, but only

           through

            its

              untelling

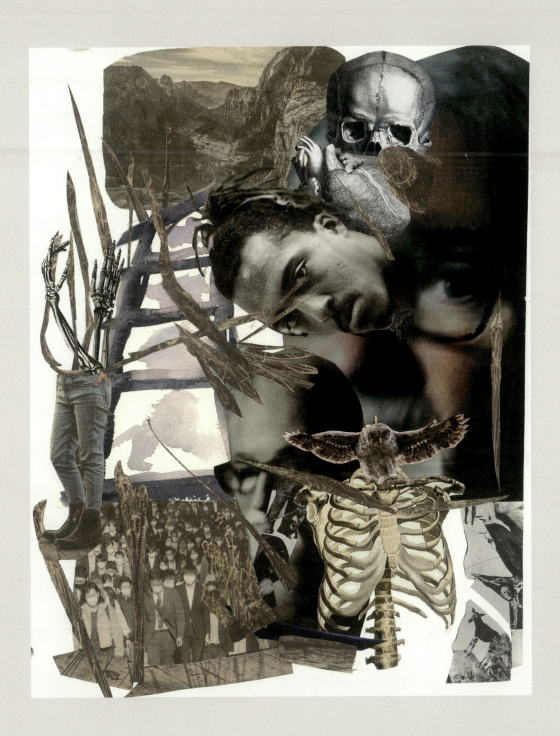

FIGURE 3.34

FIGURE 3.35

FIGURE 3.36

we do not need a
doctor to say
dance dance
dance before
the song
runs out

,

there's an ethics in this

(uncovering moral cover stories, hacking them to pieces)

                                          in this asymptotical tending
                                                                                 this
               unflinching
                      curve of tenderness   you my student taught me [[Alexa
               this griefremembering tending
          inside a dark interiority not my own   you breathing student no longer

                      holding this unholding as   teaching me now how to ask about living

               howarewetolivehowarewetolivehowarewetolive
          ungrasping ungrabbing unraveling substrate   at this endoftheworld

"She was called Alexa but believed that Antigone was her true name." Died, 25, in the midst of thinking-feeling in the midst of ethics-asking in the midst of poemlifemaking, in the midst of vast pits of disturbance.

                As Antigone is to brave, as

                Light is to shape, as

                End is to crossing, so

                X is to grief's acrostic

                Assignment.

,

(in John Ashbery's *Poems & Collages*)

—Are some of these collages autobiographical?

—Yeah, more or less. Like comic strips of

(small child)   findings in a box in an attic

frayed scraps of material
(long ago dresses, aprons, blouses, dishtowels) for

~~a quilt~~

~~or a movie~~   that has never been made

,

(Jonathan, revoiced through his daughter at his memorial service)

—Do you believe in God?

—I believe in an ancient greek god up above fuckingwithus.

andcrying welaugh

,

(sapphic couple [interracial] momentarily unglued &breaking into tears [mine not hers])

—Why are you crying?

—Because i'm a Weepy White Woman (capital W thricerolled)

The Crying Book c'est moi

thenwelaugh

,

(same sapphic couple, silver screen, in the dark)

—What's the role of black people in movies?

—To help white people get in touch with their feelings.

,

each one sends her arrow into the target of the other

FIGURE 3.37 (*top*) and FIGURE 3.38 (*bottom*)

FIGURE 3.39 (*top*) and FIGURE 3.40 (*bottom*)

,

(same couple)

We joke about W ^{thricerolled} and our common refrain about black people in movies

^{joke}funnynotfunny

remembering Cheryl Dunye's *Watermelon Woman*   those   *Plantation Memories*

black people (beastofburden) bearing whitefeeling in films   & in life

(blackbackbreakinglabor)

no: tongue breaks and thins
fire is racing under skin
and in eyes no sight and drumming
  fills ears

pretty pretty such a pretty pretty pretty girl ♪

FIGURE 3.41

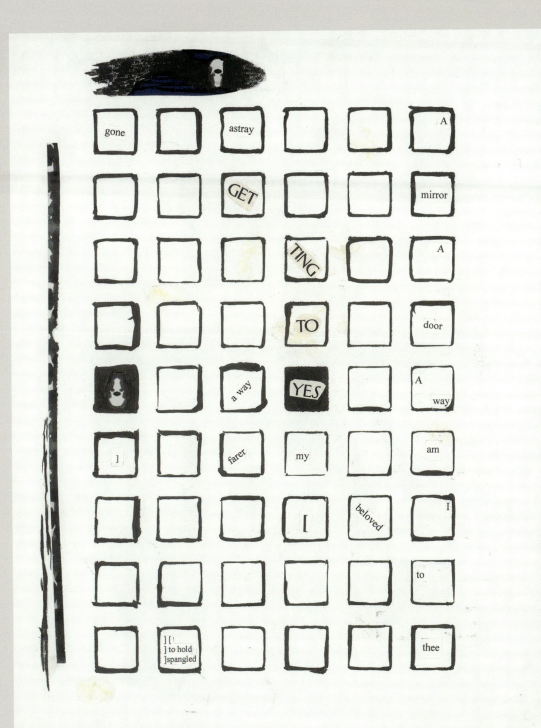

FIGURE 3.42

FIGURE 3.43 (*top*) and FIGURE 3.44 (*bottom*)

,

(same couple)

]
] longing
]

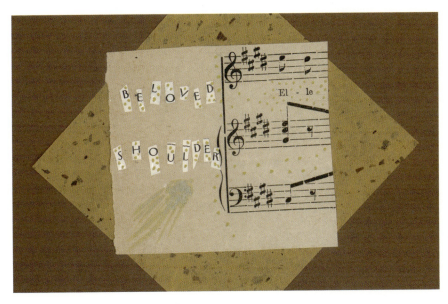

FIGURE 3.45

missing breath
marks

breath taken

breath held

breathless
beauty

,

and your comet, a birthmark

        a remembering of   those Hubble photographs (after Sappho)

pictures of you

        dug up from an archive of

                star clusters

      fireworks   whirligigs

    spirals   arcs   eagles

  pinwheels   bubbles   horseheads

    sombreros   butterflies

    mystic mountains   pillars

        eyes of God

Dust & gas gathered after ten billion light-years, then
        comet made flesh

                        ex-static

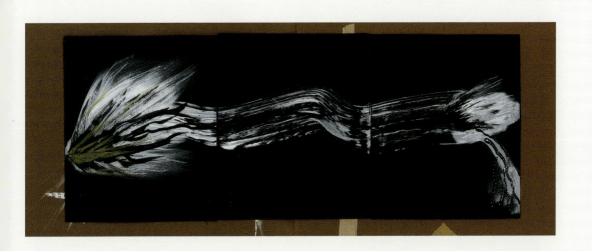

FIGURE 3.46

FIGURE 3.47

FIGURE 3.48

,

Proust placard rolled in a tube no longer legible   &whitewoodsfur in a tube

I know that smell

like a paintbrush or Proust-ended blade for beheading

FIGURE 3.49

la patte du peintre

,

(after someone at an aa meeting suddenly recognized my author name [so much for anonymity] and someone else asked)

are you famous?

andwelaughed

what is an author?
what does it matter
who is speaking?

,

Collaging the practice of a childlike mind.

                Mind   t
                          u
                                r
                            n
                    i
              n
       g

like the mind of a newcaught animal.
Childmind s
          c   t
     a   t   r   mind
        e

                    thoughtfeeling mind everyday minded minding of the
ills of a planet or just
    a gaggle or a crowd or a flock (holding on) or a herd (dying)   [species Xtinguishing
                                                                                      impossible to see
              Childminded mind an adult growing down   how to everyday
                          losing words   mind
                      [Wah I'm speechless]   this
but heart still full   to   Xtinction?]
                                            over
                                                  f
                                                      l
                                                          o
                                                                     w i n g

But Dawn stood speechless at the last gate, for as she
looked at the old friends beside her and the new ones before
her, her heart was full to overflowing, and her thoughts, like
the world about her, were golden with the joy of a new day.

FIGURE 3.50

FIGURE 3.51

,

          When day comes we step out of the shade,
                aflame and unafraid.

Cadence, *cadere*, to fall.
Rhythm of her voice: find light there, now, in a youth
                          poet
                                   laureate's cadence

        brave enough to see it
            . . . brave enough to be it.

]
]

    just now goldsandaled Dawn

    spangled is
    the earth with her crowns

    ] [
    ] to hold
    ] spangled

and I notsofamous (unlike inaugurating sweetpoetvoice)
        I-speech scatters
            becoming speechless at the gate
                    another day

cracking open an empty page
picking up pen   knife&glue   or strange fur-tufted Proust-tube for painting or beheading

& lodging myself (everscattering)   in the breach (bonevalleyed)

                      in the middles
                      in the darks

           (with others whispering, idiorrhythmic)

these survivals gathering as I pause

                                                    WahI'mspeechless

                      arrows flown

                  missed buttonholes

                                                    allthatbreathes

slender gaps in allthose paths of speech

                                            light strands and dark strands

                         [[

                flying, fluttering, breathing this earth

                      my darling one

]

                    ἐκπεποταμένα

FIGURE 3.52

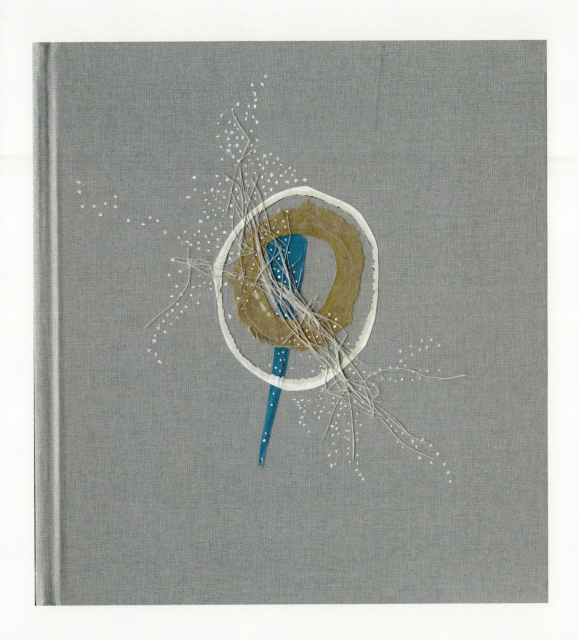

FIGURE 3.53

FIGURE 3.54

FIGURE 3.55

FIGURE 3.56

FIGURE 3.57

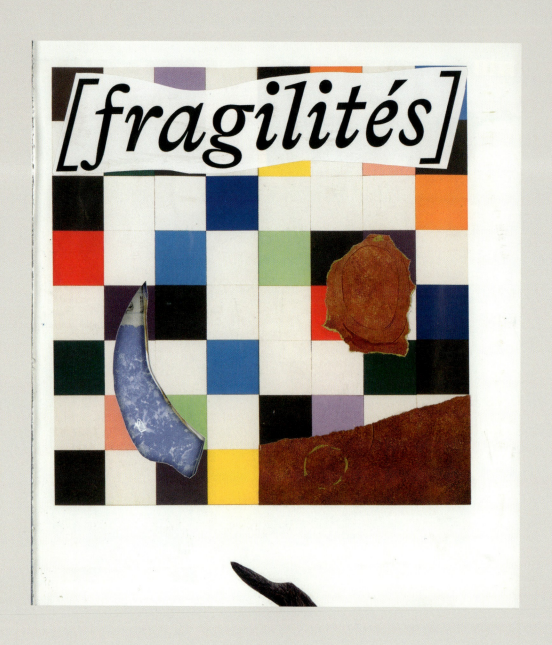

FIGURE 3.58

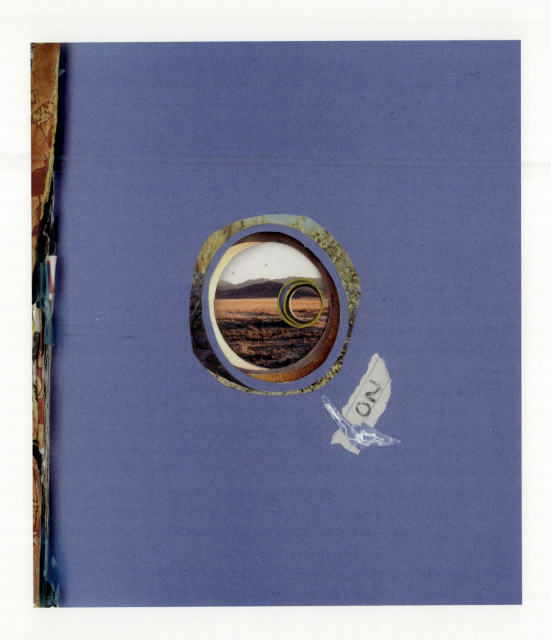

FIGURE 3.59

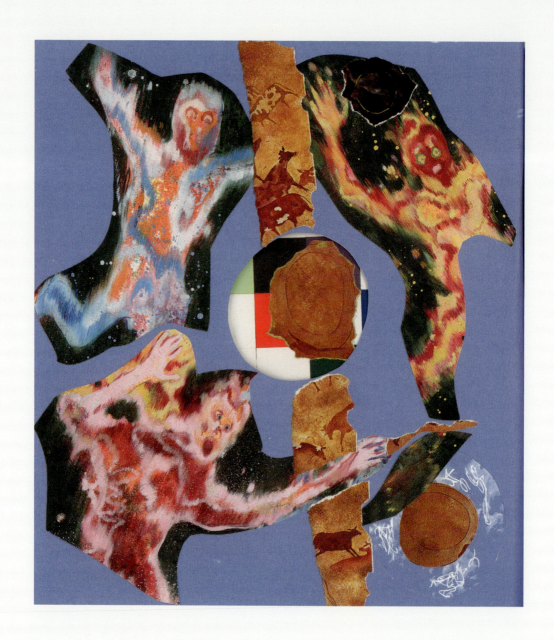

FIGURE 3.60

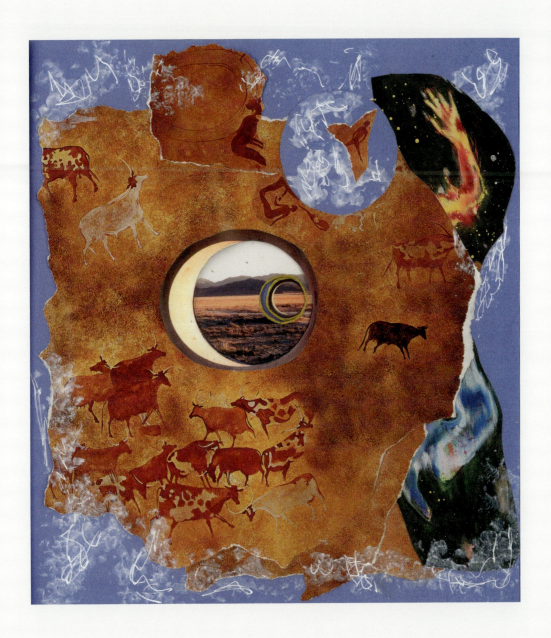

FIGURE 3.61

FIGURE 3.62

FIGURE 3.63

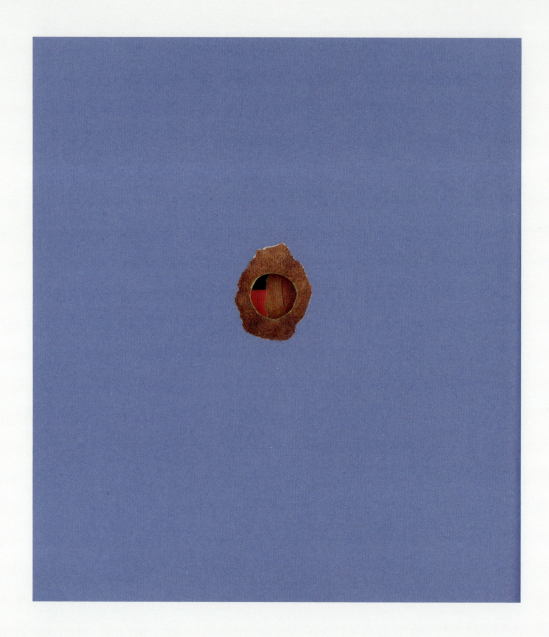

FIGURE 3.64

FIGURE 3.65

FIGURE 3.66

CODA

(comingback fragment)

OTOTOI POPO DA!

FIGURE C.1

APPENDICES

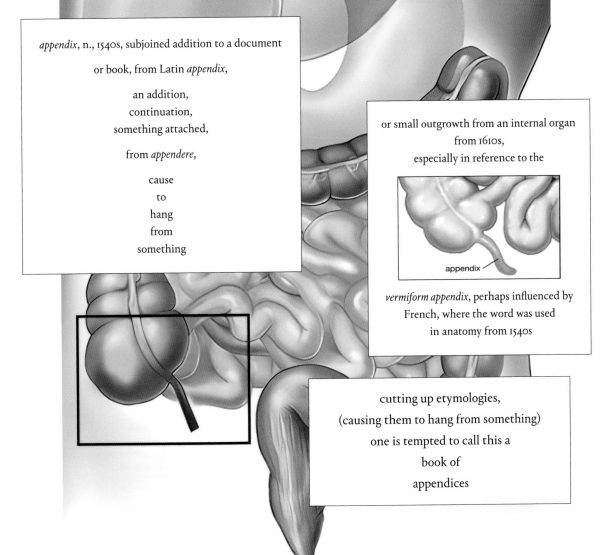

appendix, n., 1540s, subjoined addition to a document
or book, from Latin *appendix*,
an addition,
continuation,
something attached,
from *appendere*,
cause
to
hang
from
something

or small outgrowth from an internal organ
from 1610s,
especially in reference to the

vermiform appendix, perhaps influenced by
French, where the word was used
in anatomy from 1540s

cutting up etymologies,
(causing them to hang from something)
one is tempted to call this a
book of
appendices

APPENDIX I

A Note on ~~Method~~ (Training)

This book of fragments was over ten years in the making. It was finally finished in May 2023, at the end of a year in scholar's paradise, the Institute for Advanced Study in Princeton. In the end all these fragments, and many more, were strung on lines across my IAS apartment. They needed the laundry lines and clothespins for movement in space, enough to find a shape that might hold. The space where the fragments hung was also a domestic space for cooking, eating, sleeping, stretching, reading, collaging, writing, bathing, crying, laughing, spacing out, listening, talking with friends. Over time my living space became an accidental art installation, a beautiful monster that left me gawking and speechless. Months and months of daily living inside a three-dimensional collage made visible things otherwise not seen, like looking at what I'd made from the inside out rather than standing outside it. It felt like I had physically taken up residence inside my own head, where I became nothing more or less than a puzzle piece in a chaos of pieces. Gradually the book began to form and, *in the end*, as with a puzzle, the *last* pieces suddenly snapped into place (*in the end* and *last* in italics to mark them as temporary fictions: fragments will scatter, after all, beginning again).

The book's relatively slow formation is not a source of regret: it needed time. During my overadecade of living with fragments other books were written, mostly in the language of the learned intellectual (listed in appendix III). Those books have their uses. But (I now see, only now) this is the one I was after. Over the years, a philosophical interest in fragments led me down some mind-bending paths, followed but not published. Written out, rewritten, fussed over again and again, occasionally presented to others, most of that philosophical webbing has been excised from the book. But the thinking opened up by those hours of (useless?) rumination (what is a fragment? what is a whole? the Pali word for this is *papañcha*)—this "effusion of mental commentary," as Bikkhu Bodhi puts it—has now settled into the book's (mostly invisible) substrate.

Happily, playfully, I think of this as a book of training, inspired by Oulipo, poets, hybrid writers, and practitioners of verbal, visual, sonic, bodily experiments everywhere, devotees of what Annette Gilbert calls *Literature's Elsewheres*. Like Gilbert, I have come to experience these practices in constraint and assemblage as necessary (food and water) for living.

Over the course of my long habitation with fragments, my concentration on them came and went. I liken that erratic attention to what Proust calls "the intermittences of the heart," a cryptic otherness within the self that relentlessly distorts the mirror of her life. The closer she looks, the more her own self-image dissolves (along with the image she holds of those who surround and inhabit her). The film I am constantly making in my own head about the particular life I'm living is fragile, segmented, interrupted: radical montage. Both the fragments between the cuts and the cuts themselves can be riveting at times, at other times boring, but they won't coalesce into something fully known or recognized, no matter how long they hang out together. Living joyfully with a picture of a life grown stranger and stranger as time passes (not quite growing up, growing sideways) requires patience and diligent practice (meditation). Most acutely, the final snapshot (a book) will forever resist completion because its beat is the heart's intermittence. Static form will betray it (even this joyfully cut-up, cut-out, cat-rubbing collage with movable parts).

On collage. With a few exceptions, this book's collages-inside-a-collage and altered books-inside-a-book were made by me (see appendix IV). In 2016 a fascist buffoon (a joke that kills) was elected to the office of the US presidency. In 2020 COVID-19 upended everything. Intuitively, in the dark, with fingers fumbling for the light switch (*tâtonnement*), I started cutting and pasting. Unexpectedly, distress and upheaval opened up a new creative mode. Breathtaken, breath-held breathlessness suddenly felt like art: breath marks. Collaging, mostly inside large black-bound sketchbooks I had been using for years for journaling, was enhanced by other bookmaking activities: accordion folds, pop-ups, text-and-letter imaging, cutouts, tunnels, altered books. All of these practices became survival tools for living.

On ~~method~~. In his 1977 Collège de France lecture course, *How to Live Together*, Roland Barthes contrasts method with culture as training. Method is "the straight path" that "enters into the service of a generality, a 'morality.'" Like the older Barthes in his self-undoing dotage, I have come to prefer radical obliquities to the straight line. Resisting method, in his 1977 course Barthes instead invokes training (the *paideia* of the Greeks), "a kind of *dispatching* along an eccentric path: stumbling among snatches, between the bounds of different fields of knowledge, flavors." Such eccentricities are not exercises in solipsism. The stumbling happens with others, soundings in a collective beat Barthes calls idiorrhythmy (*idios*, particular, plus *rhuthmos*, rhythm): a practice of solitude in the midst of communal life. This book reflects my own idiorrhythmic need for solitude in community. Fragments mark the tug of that often wrenching need: its conflicts and difficulties, its passions and disappointments. Fragments know that living together isn't easy, but without the others-welove there would be no collage. Welove is its glue, what allows it to find a shape worth making.

This book is thick with the words of others, what Julia Kristeva once called a "mosaic of quotations." Those words have lived in me for years. Putting them on the page is a way of honoring that weave of voices and acknowledging my dependence on them, this community of academic monastics, along with a gaggle of wild heretics, beloved beasts, and feral family. I suspect many who live most deeply in me will remain unvoiced here. They live more quietly in my bones. In those empty spaces, those places where a thought might be but isn't (call it freedom), those line breaks that separate the fragments. Slender gaps, breath marks in paths of speech. No listing of sources can do them justice.

APPENDIX II

Sources (Citations)

Numbers refer to pages where citations occur. Each page number is followed by an abridgment of the relevant citation and source. More complete bibliographic information for each source can be found in appendix III.

ix   "but what was scattered": Heraclitus, Fragments.

I. FRAGMENTS COMINGBACK

3   "Coda Sapphic": Huffer, *Foucault's Strange Eros*.
4   "One day, perhaps": Foucault, "Madness, the Absence of an Oeuvre."
4   "ἐκπεποταμένα": Sappho fragment 55 in Carson, *If Not, Winter*.
5   "poem lives": Foucault, "Lives of Infamous Men."
5   *"what is black"*: Shockley, *Suddenly We*.
5   "wish my pussy": Parker, "Hottentot Venus."
8   "miniaturized collapse" and "A vanitas image": Bruyère, *Environmental Humanities*.
9   "words are coined": Carson, *An Oresteia*.
9   "dayvisible," "lightbringing," "purplepaved": Aiskhylos, *Agamemnon*.
9   "the time of madness" and "the time of unreason": Foucault, *History of Madness*.
11   "a piece of meteor": Blanchot, "Fragment-Word."
11   "it is the fragment": Tronzo, "Introduction," in *The Fragment*.
11   *"what is black"*: Shockley, *Suddenly We*.
11   "Purifoyed dada junkyard": Sirmans and Lipschutz, *Noah Purifoy: Junk Dada*.
12   "speaks more truthfully": Adorno, *Minima Moralia*.
12   "renewed possibility": Tsing, "Patchy Anthropocene."
15   "It is the whole": Tronzo, "Introduction," in *The Fragment*.
17   "We admire a text": Gallop (citing Barthes), *The Deaths of the Author*.
17   "Wearing nothing but a shirt": Foucault, *Discipline and Punish*.
17   "be consumed by fire": Foucault, *Discipline and Punish*.
20   "Oh she's mad": Aiskhylos, *Agamemnon*.
20   *"A Drowned World?"* and "Paleozoic Past": Ballard, *The Drowned World*.
20   "We like nonfiction": Shields, *Reality Hunger*.
20   "with her language that breaks open": Carson, *An Oresteia*.
20   "ΟΤΟΤΟΙ POPOI DA!": Aiskhylos, *Agamemnon*.
20   "For her way of turning": Aiskhylos, *Agamemnon*.
21   "using watercolour, pencil": Mills, "Choosing Paper for a Substrate."

41	"sees it truly," "no one ever believes," and "ungraspable": Carson, *An Oresteia*.
41	"shimmers, billows," "sliding," and "Segmented Essay" instructions: Panning, "Paper Clips."
42	"she was taken": Connolly, "Young Girl Believed Taken by Crocodile."
43	"These serpents slay men": Mandeville, *The Travels of Sir John Mandeville*.
43	"canceling-out effect," "In the midst of," and "absences, lacunae": Green, "Survival."
43	"that which is beyond understanding": Green, "Survival."
43	"the *unbearable*": Wendy Brown over lunch at the IAS.
44	"if you're lying down": Medhanandi, "The Threads of Your Life."
44	"thinking resembles tracking": Robertson (quoting Arendt), *Nilling*.
44	"I deny morality": Nietzsche, *Daybreak*.
45	"gray, meticulous": Foucault, "Nietzsche, Genealogy, History."
45	"infinite regress": Sells, *Mystical Languages of Unsaying*.
46	"moral gives cover": Joan Wallach Scott, private correspondence.
47	"suitcase under a bed": Lewis, *To the Realization of Perfect Helplessness*.
47	"philosopher's love letters": Foucault to Jean Barraqué in Huffer, *Mad for Foucault*.
47	"collage's parts always seem": Shields, *Reality Hunger*.
48	"*Recordar*": Galeano, *The Book of Embraces*.
58	"Knowledge is made for cutting": Foucault, "Nietzsche, Genealogy, History."
59	"the vile sovereign": Foucault, *Abnormal*.
59	"the violence of paint": Francis Bacon in Carson, *An Oresteia*.
59	"movedonherlikeabitch": Trump, "Transcript."
60	"grabembythepussyyoucandoanything": Trump, "Transcript."
60	"*souveraineté infâme*": Foucault, *Les Anormaux*.
60	"crimsoncovered," "purplepaved," "redsaturated," "rawflesheating lion": Aiskhylos, *Agamemnon*.
61	"Père Ubu": Jarry, *Ubu roi*.
61	"administrative grotesque": Foucault, *Abnormal*.
64	"An investigation is like an onion": Fani Willis in Hakim and Fausset, "In Georgia, a New District Attorney."
64	"murdering the text": Philip, *Zong!*
64	"A defiance of authority": Howe, *Spontaneous Particulars*.
64	"Outside, makeshift gallows": "Capitol Riot," *Tampa Bay Times*.
64	"All night long": Sappho fragment 3 in Carson, *If Not, Winter*.
64	"To *break* into tears," "into the nation of cry": Christle, *The Crying Book*.
64	"language that breaks open": Carson, *An Oresteia*.
66	"Many members of Congress": Lois Frankel in Man, "Ted Deutch Joins Push."
67	"Beautiful thing! aflame": Williams, *Paterson*.
69	"[You for] the fragrant-bosomed": West, "A New Sappho Poem."
69	"there is a space": Carson, "The Art of Poetry."
69	"] the fragrant-bosomed": Carson, *If Not, Winter*.
71	"Oh that I had wings": Psalms 55:6, King James Bible Online.
71	"What is God's will for a wing?": Teresa of Avila, *The Collected Works*.
71	"the sub sub librarian": Howe, *Spontaneous Particulars*.
72	"my looking-glass hands": Howe, *Spontaneous Particulars*.
74	"Genealogy is gray": Foucault, "Nietzsche, Genealogy, History."

II. IN THE MIDDLE, IN THE DARK, BETWEEN US

82   "one of the soldiers": John 19:34, King James Bible Online.
84   "the most erotic place *onthebody*": Barthes, *Le Plaisir du texte*, my translation.
84   "where the garment gapes?," "*là où le vêtement baille?*": Barthes, *Le Plaisir du texte*.
85   "Nietzsche's blond beasts": Nietzsche, *On the Genealogy of Morals*.
86   "mystic hystericized": Irigaray, "La Mystérique."
86   "*la mystérique c'est moi*": Huffer, "Mysterics."
89   "the violence of paint": Francis Bacon in Carson, *An Oresteia*.
89   "the best day of my life—my rebirthday, so to speak": Harding, *On Having No Head*.
89   "a-lethia": Heidegger, "The Origin of the Work of Art."
93   "a difference you cannot grasp" and "a glass": Carson, *An Oresteia*.
93   "overseeing": Wynter, "Unsettling the Coloniality of Being."
93   "pornotroping": Spillers, "Mama's Baby, Papa's Maybe."
93   "knowing it too much": Foucault, *History of Madness*.
93   "*un rien-à-voir*": Irigaray, *Speculum of the Other Woman*.
97   "in the beginning": Foucault, "Nietzsche, Genealogy, History."
97   "In Delhi": Sen, *All That Breathes*.
97   "griefremembering": Aiskhylos, *Agamemnon*.
97   "bone, mummy, ash, soil": Povinelli, *Geontologies*.
97   "time of unreason": Foucault, *History of Madness*.
97   "wings flying fluttering": Carson, *If Not, Winter*.
99   "Eros is a verb": Carson, *Eros the Bittersweet*.
100   "Ecstasy is there": Irigaray, "La Mystérique."
101   "vestibular": Spillers, "Mama's Baby, Papa's Maybe."
101   "*le réseau carcéral*": Foucault, *Surveiller et punir*.
101   "just an asymptotical tending": Cucopulos, "Poiesis and Death."
101   "this dark interiority that isn't my own": Cucopulos, "Poiesis and Death."
102   "*what is black*" and "suddenly we": Shockley, *Suddenly We*.
102   "a difference we cannot grasp" and "a glass": Carson, *An Oresteia*.

III. DÉCOLLAGE

107   "like a cat": Blofeld, "A Spirit of Reverence."
108   "she learned the key to everything": Boyer, *Garments against Women*.
130   "probably more meaningful": Boyer, *Garments against Women*.
132   "forms (nouns) do not matter in themselves": Blofeld, "A Spirit of Reverence."
139   "One day perhaps": Foucault, "Madness, the Absence of an Oeuvre."
141   Weather Reports exercise, from Sheffield's "Generative Measures" workshop.
143   "murder the text" and "Zong! is the Song": Philip, *Zong!*
143   "in the break": Moten, *In the Break*.
143   "a single square bracket": Carson, *If Not, Winter*.
144   "a blizzard of marks": Carson, *If Not, Winter*.
144   "cannot be told yet must be told": Philip, *Zong!*
147   "we do not need a doctor": Conrad, "Listen to the Golden Boomerang Return."

148	"She was called Alexa": Bennett, "Instructor's Note."
149	Ashbery dialogue, Ashbery, *They Knew What They Wanted*.
153	"each one sends her arrow into the target of the other": Deleuze in Huffer, "Twisted."
156	"no: tongue breaks and thins": Sappho fragment in Carson, *If Not, Winter*.
156	"pretty pretty such a": Rolling Stones, "Beast of Burden."
159	"] longing]": Sappho fragment in Carson, *If Not, Winter*.
160	"Hubble photographs (after Sappho)": Rich, "Hubble Photographs (After Sappho)."
160	"ex-static": Rich, "Hubble Photographs (After Sappho)."
164	"Proust placard rolled in a tube": Williams, "Paperoles"
165	"what does it matter": Foucault, "What Is an Author?"
167	"But Dawn stood speechless": Smith, *Molly's Miracle*.
169	"When day comes we step out of the shade": Gorman, *The Hill We Climb*.
169	"just now goldsandaled Dawn": Sappho fragment 123 in Carson, *If Not, Winter*.
169	"spangled is / the earth with her crowns": Sappho fragment 168d in Carson, *If Not, Winter*.
169	"to hold / spangled": Sappho fragment 98b in Carson, *If Not, Winter*.
170	"allthatbreathes": Sen, *All That Breathes*.
170	"slender gaps": Foucault, *The Archeology of Knowledge*.
170	"light strands and dark strands": Rumi, "The Diver's Clothes Lying Empty on the Beach."
170	"flying, fluttering": Carson, *If Not, Winter*.
170	"my darling one": Sappho fragment 163 in Carson, *If Not, Winter*.
170	"ἐκπεποταμένα": Sappho fragment 55 in Carson, *If Not, Winter*.
174	"the world keeps ending": Choi, *The World Keeps Ending*.

APPENDIX I. A NOTE ON ~~METHOD~~ (TRAINING)

193	"effusion of mental commentary": Bikkhu Bodhi quoted in Olendzki, "What Is Papañca?"
193	"the intermittences of the heart": Proust, *Sodom and Gomorrah*.
194	"a joke that kills": Foucault, *Abnormal*.
194	"*tâtonnement*": Deleuze in Huffer, "Twisted."
194	"straight path": Barthes, *How to Live Together*.
194	"a kind of *dispatching*": Barthes, *How to Live Together*.
194	"a mosaic of quotations": Kristeva, "Word, Dialogue and Novel."
194	"slender gaps, breath marks in paths of speech": Foucault, *The Archeology of Knowledge*.

APPENDIX III

Substrate (Works Cited)

Adorno, Theodor. *Minima Moralia: Reflections from Damaged Life*. Translated by Edmund F. N. Jephcott. London: Verso, 2020.

Aiskhylos. *Agamemnon*. In *An Oresteia*, translated by Anne Carson. London: Faber and Faber, 2010.

Ashbery, John. *They Knew What They Wanted: Collages and Poems*. New York: Rizzoli Electa, 2018.

Ballard, J. G. *The Drowned World*. New York: Liveright, 2023.

Barthes, Roland. *How to Live Together: Novelistic Simulations of Some Everyday Spaces. Notes for a Lecture Course and Seminar at the Collège de France (1976–1977)*. Translated by Kate Briggs. New York: Columbia University Press, 2013.

Barthes, Roland. *Le Plaisir du texte*. Paris: Seuil, 1982.

Bennett, Amanda. "Instructor's Note." In *Desideratum: The Pieces of Us*, 2021. Accessed February 17, 2024. https://issuu.com/celinexwei/docs/desideratum_the_pieces_of_us.

Blanchot, Maurice. "Fragment-Word." In *The Infinite Conversation*, translated by Susan Hanson, 307–13. Minneapolis: University of Minnesota Press, 1993.

Blofeld, John. "A Spirit of Reverence." *Tricycle: The Buddhist Review* (Spring 2016). https://tricycle.org/magazine/spirit-reverence/.

Boyer, Anne. *Garments against Women*. New York: Penguin, 2019.

Bruyère, Vincent. *Environmental Humanities on the Brink: The Vanitas Hypothesis*. Palo Alto: Stanford University Press, 2023.

"Capitol Riot More Sinister Than It Looked as Gallows, Pipes, and Guns Turn Up." *Tampa Bay Times*, January 11, 2021. https://www.tampabay.com/news/florida-politics/2021/01/11/capitol-riot-more-sinister-that-it-looked-as-gallows-pipes-and-guns-turn-up/.

Carson, Anne. "The Art of Poetry No. 88." *Paris Review* 46, no. 171 (Fall 2004): 190–226.

Carson, Anne. *Eros the Bittersweet*. Princeton, NJ: Princeton University Press, 1986.

Carson, Anne. *If Not, Winter: Fragments of Sappho*. New York: Random House, 2002.

Carson, Anne, trans. *An Oresteia*. London: Faber and Faber, 2010.

Choi, Franny. *The World Keeps Ending and the World Goes On*. New York: Ecco, 2022.

Christle, Heather. *The Crying Book*. New York: Catapult, 2019.

Connolly, Ellen. "Young Girl Believed Taken by Crocodile in Australia." *World*, November 16, 2012. https://theworld.org/stories/2012-11-16/young-girl-believed-taken-crocodile-australia.

Conrad, CA. "Listen to the Golden Boomerang Return." 1966. Accessed February 17, 2024. https://poets.org/poem/listen-golden-boomerang-return.

Cucopulos, Alexa. "Poiesis and Death: Foucault's Chiastic Undoing of Life in *History of Sexuality Volume One*." Honors thesis, Emory University, 2016.

Easter, Makeda. "The Broad's 'Soul of a Nation': Art from the Rubble of Watts." *Los Angeles Times*, March 22, 2019. https://www.latimes.com/entertainment/arts/la-et-cm-soul-nation-art-black-power-broad-20190322-story.html.

Foucault, Michel. *Abnormal: Lectures at the Collège de France, 1974–1975*. Translated by Graham Burchell. New York: Picador, 2003.

Foucault, Michel. *"The Archeology of Knowledge" and "The Discourse on Language."* Translated by Alan Sheridan. New York: Pantheon, 1982.

Foucault, Michel. *Discipline and Punish: The Birth of the Prison*. Translated by Alan Sheridan. New York: Random House, 1977.

Foucault, Michel. *History of Madness*. Translated by Jonathan Murphy and Jean Khalfa. London: Routledge, 2006.

Foucault, Michel. *Les Anormaux: Cours au Collège de France, 1974-1975*. Paris: Gallimard, 1999.

Foucault, Michel. "Lives of Infamous Men." In *Essential Works of Foucault, 1954-1984*, edited by Paul Rabinow, 3 vols., 3:157-75. New York: New Press, 2000.

Foucault, Michel. "Madness, the Absence of an Oeuvre." In *History of Madness*, translated by Jonathan Murphy and Jean Khalfa, 541-49. London: Routledge, 2006.

Foucault, Michel. "Nietzsche, Genealogy, History." In *Essential Works of Foucault, 1954-1984*, edited by Paul Rabinow, 3 vols., 2:369-92. New York: New Press, 1998.

Foucault, Michel. *Surveiller et punir: Naissance de la prison*. Paris: Gallimard, 1975.

Foucault, Michel. "What Is an Author?" In *Essential Works of Foucault, 1954-1984*, edited by Paul Rabinow, 3 vols., 1:303-20. New York: New Press, 1998.

Galeano, Eduardo. *The Book of Embraces*. Translated by Cedric Belfrage. New York: Norton, 1992.

Gallop, Jane. *The Deaths of the Author: Reading and Writing in Time*. Durham, NC: Duke University Press, 2011.

Gilbert, Annette. *Literature's Elsewheres: On the Necessity of Radical Literary Practices*. Cambridge, MA: MIT Press, 2022.

Gorman, Amanda. *The Hill We Climb: An Inaugural Poem for the Country*. New York: Viking, 2021.

Green, Renée. "Survival: Ruminations on Archival Lacunae." 2001. In *Other Planes of There: Selected Writings*, 271-88. Durham, NC: Duke University Press, 2014.

Hakim, Danny, and Richard Fausset. "In Georgia, a New District Attorney Starts Circling Trump and His Allies." *New York Times*, February 13, 2021. https://www.nytimes.com/2021/02/13/us/politics/fani-willis-trump.html.

Harding, D. E. *On Having No Head: Zen and the Rediscovery of the Obvious*. London: Shollond Trust, 2014.

Heidegger, Martin. "The Origin of the Work of Art." In *Poetry, Language, Thought*, translated by Albert Hofstadter, 15-88. New York: Harper and Row, 1971.

Heraclitus. *Fragments*. Translated by Brooks Haxton. New York: Penguin, 2003.

Howe, Susan. *Spontaneous Particulars: The Telepathy of Archives*. New York: New Directions, 2014.

Huffer, Lynne. *Another Colette: The Question of Gendered Writing*. Ann Arbor: University of Michigan Press, 1992.

Huffer, Lynne. *Are the Lips a Grave? A Queer Feminist on the Ethics of Sex*. New York: Columbia University Press, 2013.

Huffer, Lynne. *Foucault's Strange Eros*. New York: Columbia University Press, 2020.

Huffer, Lynne. *Mad for Foucault: Rethinking the Foundations of Queer Theory*. New York: Columbia University Press, 2010.

Huffer, Lynne. *Maternal Pasts, Feminist Futures: Nostalgia, Ethics, and the Question of Difference*. Stanford: Stanford University Press, 1998.

Huffer, Lynne. "Mysterics: Extinction and Emptiness." In *What Is Sexual Difference? Thinking with Irigaray*, edited by Mary C. Rawlinson and James Sares, 372-426. New York: Columbia University Press, 2023.

Huffer, Lynne. "Twisted (A Tribute): Foucault, Deleuze, and the Rhizomatic Book." In *The Politics of Desire: Foucault, Deleuze, and Psychoanalysis*, edited by Agustín Colombo, Edward McGushin, and Geoff Pfeifer, 101-20. London: Rowman and Littlefield, 2022.

Irigaray, Luce. "La Mystérique." In *Speculum de l'autre femme*, 238-52. Paris: Minuit, 1974.

Irigaray, Luce. *Speculum of the Other Woman*. Translated by Gillian C. Gill. Ithaca, NY: Cornell University Press, 1985.

Jarry, Alfred. *Ubu roi*. Paris: Livre de poche, 2000.

King James Bible Online. Accessed February 17, 2024. https://www.kingjamesbibleonline.org.

Kristeva, Julia. "Word, Dialogue and Novel." In *The Kristeva Reader*, edited by Toril Moi, 34-61. New York: Columbia University Press, 1986.

Lewis, Robin Coste. *To the Realization of Perfect Helplessness*. New York: Knopf, 2022.

Man, Anthony. "Ted Deutch Joins Push to Expel QAnon-Promoter Marjorie Taylor Greene from Congress." *Sun Sentinel*, January 29, 2021. https://www.sun-sentinel.com/2021/01/28/ted-deutch-joins-push-to-expel-qanon-promoter-marjorie-taylor-greene-from-congress/.

Mandeville, John. *The Travels of Sir John Mandeville*. New York: Penguin, 2005.

Medhanandi, Ayya. "The Threads of Your Life: Guided Death Meditation." Dharma Seed, March 11, 2007. https://dharmaseed.org/talks/54359/.

Mills, Marilyn Harris. "Choosing Paper for a Substrate." Mixed Media Art. Accessed August 27, 2024. https://www.mixedmediaart.net/mixed-media-materials/choosing-paper-substrate.

Moten, Fred. *In the Break: The Aesthetics of the Black Radical Tradition*. Minneapolis: University of Minnesota Press, 2003.

Nietzsche, Friedrich. *Daybreak: Thoughts on the Prejudices of Morality*. Edited by Maudemarie Clark and Brian Leiter. Translated by R. J. Hollingdale. Cambridge: Cambridge University Press, 1997.

Nietzsche, Friedrich. *"On the Genealogy of Morals" and "Ecce Homo."* Translated by Walter Kaufmann. New York: Vintage, 1969.

Olendzki, Andrew. "What Is Papañca?" *Lion's Roar*, 2006. Accessed February 17, 2024. https://www.lionsroar.com/what-is-papanca/.

Panning, Ann. "Paper Clips, Sausage, Candy Cigarettes, Silk: 'Thingy-ness' in Flash Nonfiction." In *The Rose Metal Press Field Guide to Writing Flash Nonfiction: Advice and Essential Exercises from Respected Writers, Editors, and Teachers*, edited by Dinty W. Moore, 37–42. Brookline, MA: Rose Metal, 2012.

Parker, Morgan. "Hottentot Venus." In *There Are More Beautiful Things than Beyoncé*, 6–7. New York: Tin House Books, 2017.

Philip, M. NourbeSe. *Zong! As Told to the Author by Setaey Adamu Boateng*. Middletown, CT: Wesleyan University Press, 2011.

Povinelli, Elizabeth. *Geontologies: A Requiem to Late Liberalism*. Durham, NC: Duke University Press, 2016.

Proust, Marcel. *Sodom and Gomorrah*. Translated by John Sturrock. Vol. 4 of *In Search of Lost Time*. New York: Penguin, 2005.

Rich, Adrienne. "Hubble Photographs (After Sappho)." In *Collected Poems: 1950–2012*, 1001–2. New York: Norton, 2016.

Robertson, Lisa. *Nilling: Prose Essays on Noise, Pornography, the Codex, Melancholy, Lucretius, Folds, Cities and Related Aporias*. Toronto: Book*hug Press, 2012.

Rolling Stones. "Beast of Burden" (remastered 1994). *Some Girls*, 1978. Accessed February 17, 2024. https://www.youtube.com/watch?v=RlV-ZFyVH3c.

Rumi. "The Diver's Clothes Lying Empty on the Beach." In *The Essential Rumi*, translated by Coleman Barks. New York: Castle Books, 1995.

Sells, Michael. *Mystical Languages of Unsaying*. Chicago: University of Chicago Press, 1994.

Sen, Shaunak. *All That Breathes*. Documentary, 2022.

Sheffield, Ellen. "Generative Measures" workshop (online). Center for Book Arts, New York, Fall 2021.

Shields, David. *Reality Hunger: A Manifesto*. New York: Vintage, 2011.

Shockley, Evie. *Suddenly We*. Middletown, CT: Wesleyan University Press, 2023.

Sirmans, Franklin, and Yael Lipschutz. *Noah Purifoy: Junk Dada*. Munich: Prestel, 2015.

Smith, Linell. *Molly's Miracle*. Boston: Little, Brown, 1959.

Spillers, Hortense. "Mama's Baby, Papa's Maybe: An American Grammar Book." *Diacritics* 17, no. 2 (Summer 1987): 64–81.

Teresa of Avila. *The Collected Works of St. Teresa of Avila*. Vol. 1. Translated by Otilio Rodriguez. Washington, DC: ICS, 1987.

Tronzo, William. "Introduction." In *The Fragment: An Incomplete History*, edited by William Tronzo, 1–7. Los Angeles: Getty Research Institute, 2009.

Trump, Donald. "Transcript: Donald Trump's Taped Comments about Women." *New York Times*, October 8, 2016. https://www.nytimes.com/2016/10/08/us/donald-trump-tape-transcript.html.

Tsing, Anna. "Patchy Anthropocene: The Feral Impacts of Infrastructure." Public lecture, Institute for Advanced Study, March 29, 2023. Accessed February 16, 2024. https://www.youtube.com/watch?v=Efmf77F20NM.

West, Martin. "A New Sappho Poem." *Times Literary Supplement*, June 24, 2005.

Williams, Rhiannon. "'Paperoles': Proust and the Facility of Patching." *Critical Cloth*, March 15, 2015. https://criticalcloth.wordpress.com/2015/03/15/paperoles-proust-and-the-facility-of-patching/.

Williams, William Carlos. *Paterson*. New York: New Directions, 1995.

Wynter, Sylvia. "Unsettling the Coloniality of Being/Power/Truth/Freedom: Towards the Human, After Man, Its Overrepresentation—an Argument." *CR: The New Centennial Review* 3, no. 3 (Fall 2003): 257–337.

APPENDIX IV

List of Figures

frontispiece	Lynne Huffer, *Animal Behavior*, collage in altered book, with cutouts, flaps, and accordion fold inserts, 2023, page 5, Bryn Mawr College Special Collections.
I.1	Lynne Huffer, untitled collage, 2023.
I.2	Deer skull, photograph by Anna Tsing, September 6, 2014.
I.3	Noah Purifoy, *No Contest (Bicycles)*, assemblage sculpture, Joshua Tree Outdoor Museum, 1991.
I.4	Author photograph of fossil with haiku, 2022.
I.5	Author as child with mother, photographer unknown, 1966.
I.6	Material from author's personal archive, 1970s.
I.7	Lynne Huffer, *Animal Behavior*, altered book, with cutouts, flaps, and accordion fold inserts, 2023, spine, Bryn Mawr College Special Collections.
I.8	Lynne Huffer, *Animal Behavior*, front cover.
I.9	Lynne Huffer, *Animal Behavior*, untitled collage, inside front cover.
I.10	Lynne Huffer, *Animal Behavior*, untitled collage, page 1.
I.11	Lynne Huffer, *Animal Behavior*, untitled collage, page 2.
I.12	Lynne Huffer, *Animal Behavior*, untitled collage, page 3.
I.13	Lynne Huffer, *Animal Behavior*, untitled collage, page 4.
I.14	Lynne Huffer, *Animal Behavior*, untitled collage, page 5.
I.15	Lynne Huffer, *Animal Behavior*, untitled collage, page 6.
I.16	Lynne Huffer, *Animal Behavior*, untitled collage, page 7; includes Kara Walker cutout detail from *Harper's Pictorial History of the Civil War (Annotated)*, 2005.
I.17	Lynne Huffer, *Animal Behavior*, untitled collage, page 8.
I.18	Lynne Huffer, *Animal Behavior*, untitled collage, page 9.
I.19	Lynne Huffer, *Animal Behavior*, untitled collage, page 10.
I.20	Lynne Huffer, *Animal Behavior*, untitled collage, page 11.
I.21	Lynne Huffer, *Animal Behavior*, untitled collage, page 12.
I.22	Lynne Huffer, *Animal Behavior*, untitled collage, inside back cover.
I.23	Lynne Huffer, *Animal Behavior*, untitled collage, accordion fold open (detail), inside back cover.
I.24	Lynne Huffer, *Animal Behavior*, untitled collage, accordion fold open (detail), inside back cover.
I.25	Lynne Huffer, *Animal Behavior*, back cover.
I.26	Joan Scott haiku, 2023.
I.27	Lynne Huffer, untitled hanging collage, 2022.
I.28	Eduardo Galeano, ink drawing, *The Book of Embraces*, 1992.
I.29	Lynne Huffer, untitled collage, 2022.
I.30	Lynne Huffer, untitled collage, 2022.

1.31	Lynne Huffer, untitled hanging collage, 2023.	
1.32	Hannah Höch, *Cut with the Kitchen Knife Dada through the Last Weimar Beer-Belly Cultural Epoch in Germany*, photomontage, 1919.	
1.33	*Ubu roi* publicity poster, Tin Roof, March 2018.	
1.34	Lynne Huffer, *Fani Willis* (detail), collage, 2021.	
1.35	William Buckland, *The Hyena's Den in Kirkdale Cave*, lithograph drawing, 1822.	
1.36	Lynne Huffer, *Fani Willis* (detail), collage, 2021.	
1.37	Lynne Huffer, *Fani Willis*, collage, 2021.	
1.38	Lynne Huffer, *January 6th*, collage, 2021.	
1.39	Lynne Huffer, *Black Power*, collage, 2021.	
1.40	Lynne Huffer, *Aflame*, collage, 2021.	
1.41	Lynne Huffer, untitled collage, 2020.	
1.42	Material from author's personal archive (verso), 1970s.	
1.43	Material from author's personal archive, 1970s.	
1.44	Lynne Huffer, *Help, Bunny*, collage, 2023.	
2.1	Lynne Huffer, *La Mystérique I*, collage, 2021.	
2.2	Jean le Noir, Bourgot (?), and workshop, Miniature of Christ's Side Wound and Instruments of the Passion, folio 331r, in the *Prayer Book of Bonne of Luxembourg*, before 1349, The Cloisters Collection.	
2.3	Jean le Noir, Bourgot (?), and workshop, The Crucifixion, folio 328r, in the *Prayer Book of Bonne of Luxembourg*, before 1349, The Cloisters Collection.	
2.4	Lynne Huffer, *La Mystérique I*, collage, 2021.	
2.5	Author's mother as child, photographer unknown, 1937?	
2.6	Sappho bot. Twitter (now X).	
2.7	André Masson, *Acéphale* cover, 1936.	
2.8	Lynne Huffer, *La Mystérique I* (detail), collage, 2021.	
2.9	Lynne Huffer, *Sappho bot*, collage, 2021.	
2.10	Lynne Huffer, *La Mystérique II*, collage, 2021.	
2.11	Lynne Huffer, *La Mystérique III*, collage, 2021.	
2.12	Lynne Huffer, *La Mystérique III* (detail), collage, 2021.	
3.1	Lynne Huffer, untitled hanging collage, 2023.	
3.2	Lynne Huffer, *Prostration*, handmade book with cutouts and ink, cover, 2022.	
3.3	Lynne Huffer, *Prostration*, inside cover.	
3.4	Lynne Huffer, *Prostration*, page 1.	
3.5	Lynne Huffer, *Prostration*, page 2.	
3.6	Lynne Huffer, *Prostration*, page 3.	
3.7	Lynne Huffer, *Prostration*, page 4.	
3.8	Lynne Huffer, *Prostration*, page 5.	
3.9	Lynne Huffer, *Prostration*, page 6.	
3.10	Lynne Huffer, *Prostration*, page 7.	
3.11	Lynne Huffer, *Prostration*, page 8.	
3.12	Lynne Huffer, *Prostration*, page 9.	
3.13	Lynne Huffer, *Prostration*, page 10.	
3.14	Lynne Huffer, *Prostration*, page 11.	
3.15	Lynne Huffer, *Prostration*, page 12.	

3.16	Lynne Huffer, *Prostration*, page 13.
3.17	Lynne Huffer, *Prostration*, page 14.
3.18	Lynne Huffer, *Prostration*, page 15.
3.19	Lynne Huffer, *Prostration*, page 16.
3.20	Lynne Huffer, *Prostration*, inside back cover.
3.21	Lynne Huffer, *Prostration*, back cover.
3.22	Lynne Huffer, wall-mounted fragments (detail), 2022–23.
3.23	Lynne Huffer, wall-mounted fragments, 2022–23.
3.24	Lynne Huffer, untitled hanging collage (detail), 2023.
3.25	Lynne Huffer, untitled hanging collage (detail), 2023.
3.26	Lynne Huffer, untitled hanging collage (detail), 2023.
3.27	Lynne Huffer, untitled hanging collage, 2023.
3.28	Lynne Huffer, *Chat Box*, handmade book with cutouts and ink, inside front cover, 2022.
3.29	Lynne Huffer, *Chat Box*, page 1.
3.30	Lynne Huffer, *Chat Box*, page 2.
3.31	Lynne Huffer, *Chat Box*, inside back cover.
3.32	Lynne Huffer, *Chat Box*, back cover.
3.33	Lorraine O'Grady, *Haiku Diptych* 7, from *Cutting Out CONYT* (1977/2017).
3.34	Lynne Huffer, untitled collage, 2020.
3.35	Lynne Huffer, untitled collage, 2020.
3.36	Lynne Huffer, untitled collage, 2020.
3.37	Lynne Huffer, *Each One Sends Her Arrow* (detail), collage, 2021.
3.38	Lynne Huffer, *Each One Sends Her Arrow* (detail).
3.39	Lynne Huffer, *Each One Sends Her Arrow* (detail).
3.40	Lynne Huffer, *Each One Sends Her Arrow* (detail).
3.41	Lynne Huffer, *Animal Behavior*, collage in altered book (detail), 2023, page 7, Bryn Mawr College Special Collections; includes Kara Walker cutout detail from *Harper's Pictorial History of the Civil War (Annotated)*, 2005.
3.42	Lynne Huffer, *Getting to Yes*, collage, 2022.
3.43	Lynne Huffer, untitled hanging collage, 2013/2023.
3.44	Lynne Huffer, untitled hanging collage (detail), 2013/2023.
3.45	Lynne Huffer, *Animal Behavior*, collage in altered book (detail), 2023, inside back cover, Bryn Mawr College Special Collections.
3.46	Lynne Huffer, accordion fold insert (open), *Animal Behavior*, inside back cover, Bryn Mawr College Special Collections.
3.47	Lynne Huffer, *Ex-stasis (After Sappho)* (detail), collage, 2021.
3.48	Lynne Huffer, *Ex-stasis (After Sappho)* (detail).
3.49	Lynne Huffer, *Animal Behavior*, collage in altered book (detail), 2023, page 5, Bryn Mawr College Special Collections.
3.50	Lynne Huffer, untitled hanging collage (detail), includes altered page from *Molly's Miracle*, 2013/2023.
3.51	Lynne Huffer, untitled hanging collage (detail), includes altered page from *Molly's Miracle*.

3.52	Lynne Huffer, *Pictures of Nothing*, collage in altered book, with cutouts, 2023, spine, Bryn Mawr College Special Collections.
3.53	Lynne Huffer, *Pictures of Nothing*, cover.
3.54	Lynne Huffer, *Pictures of Nothing*, collage, inside front cover.
3.55	Lynne Huffer, *Pictures of Nothing*, collage, page 1.
3.56	Lynne Huffer, *Pictures of Nothing*, collage, page 2.
3.57	Lynne Huffer, *Pictures of Nothing*, collage, page 3.
3.58	Lynne Huffer, *Pictures of Nothing*, collage, page 4.
3.59	Lynne Huffer, *Pictures of Nothing*, collage, page 5.
3.60	Lynne Huffer, *Pictures of Nothing*, collage, page 6.
3.61	Lynne Huffer, *Pictures of Nothing*, collage, page 7.
3.62	Lynne Huffer, *Pictures of Nothing*, collage, page 8.
3.63	Lynne Huffer, *Pictures of Nothing*, collage, page 9.
3.64	Lynne Huffer, *Pictures of Nothing*, collage, page 10.
3.65	Lynne Huffer, *Pictures of Nothing*, collage, inside back cover.
3.66	Lynne Huffer, *Pictures of Nothing*, back cover.
C.1	Lynne Huffer, *Animal Behavior*, collage in altered book (detail), 2023, page 5, Bryn Mawr College Special Collections.
Appendices	Appendix, medical illustrations.

ACKNOWLEDGMENTS

I think of this book as an assemblage of borrowings: a strange counter-archive that gathers together murmurs, voices, silences, shapes, shadows falling, sounds both human and not, flashes of color, stolen glances, the scent of bodies, traces of breath, the memory of touch, pages written out, erased, written over again, crinkled, folded, burned, torn, cut, collaged into new survivals. These survivals will scatter again, beyond naming.

The attempt to name is always inadequate. But here are some people and institutions I want to acknowledge with a deep bow of gratitude. First and foremost, the generous support of the Institute for Advanced Study (IAS) in Princeton allowed me to complete this book in May 2023, at the end of my fellowship year. Special gratitude goes to Wendy Brown and Timothy Mitchell for including me in their IAS Climate Crisis Politics seminar (2022–23), to the other School of Social Science faculty members Didier Fassin and Alondra Nelson, and to all my IAS colleagues during that fellowship year. Another thanks to Wendy Brown for all those walks in the woods and for teaching me how to think-feel (again). Huge thanks to Joan Scott for haiku exchanges, for dinner parties, and for plopping down on my couch with an early printout of *These Survivals*, perusing each page and finally exclaiming (before anyone else had): "This is a book!" Big thanks to Catherine Clune-Taylor, Gayle Salamon, and Christina León for so graciously welcoming me to Princeton. Thanks to Zora for accompanying me there with her blue beanbag in tow, and for teaching me about cat prostrations for survival.

I'm grateful for the energy and creativity of the IAS Experimental Writing Group that gathered twice a month in a glass-walled room in the Rubenstein Commons: Lorenzo Alunni, Hillary Angelo, Munirah Bishop, Heather Davis, Anne-Claire Defossez, Vivian Lu, and Nayanika Mathur. Your inspiration was the wind I needed in my sails. Special thanks to Miriam Harris, Laura McCune, and Munirah Bishop for steady support during the IAS year, and to Caitlin Rizzo for insights both archival and poetic. Many thanks to Anna Tsing, whose 2023 visit to the IAS stimulated crucial reflection, and who provided me with the deer skull photograph. And to Samera Esmeir: How to thank you for those repeated circles of conversation around a field under stars? Or to express my awe at the Kanafani fragments you translated and gifted to me? "Oh love, if I could only agree with you and with fate on tearing apart this sad character of the world . . . tearing it apart into small pieces . . . and building it again . . . in accordance with the wishes of our hearts."

Many thanks also to the Emory University Fox Center for Humanistic Inquiry for a year-long fellowship (2020–21) where I began to shape these fragments into a book. I am grateful to the participants in my Spring 2022 FoxCHI Ethics of Extinction seminar for your wisdom and insights: Dayne Alexander, Tirza Ben-Ezzer, Vincent Bruyère, Meike Robaard, Shiv Sharma, and Noah Taylor. I also want to thank Carla Freeman, Deboleena Roy, and the Office of the Dean of Emory College of Arts and Sciences for allowing me the two leaves required to complete this project. Many thanks to the Emory College Subvention Fund and the Lauren Berlant Fund (established to "fund the unfundable") for financial assistance to support high-quality, full-color print copies of this book.

Both the Department of Women's, Gender, and Sexuality Studies and the Department of Philosophy at Emory have been institutional homes that allowed my work to grow. Thank you to my colleagues in our now decade-old interdisciplinary Anthropocene reading group. So many of these ideas were incubated there. John Lysaker's nuanced take on what it means to flourish has expanded my thinking about ethics in countless ways. Noelle McAfee, Chair of Philosophy, offered vital institutional and collegial support. Fay Alafouzou, my teaching assistant in fall 2023, inspired me to be a better teacher as an artist-philosopher. Elizabeth Wilson is the best colleague-friend one could ever want (what would I do without you?). Many thanks to my writing groups—Leslie Harris, Ruby Lal, Gyan Pandey, and Laurie Patton—for all those years of learning how to cross and recross the creative/academic writing divide. I'm grateful to the students in my Experimental Writing in the Anthropocene courses for teaching me how to be braver in my writing. A special thanks to my Honors student Marley Goldman for the gift of wild animal bones, for a shared love of chiasmus, and for being a model of joyous creativity. A shout-out to my former graduate students, especially Debjani Bhattacharyya, Shelley Feller, Haylee Harrell, Ege Selin Islekel, Taryn Jordan, Christina León, and Suzanne Persard, for encouraging me to be weird and for providing such stunning examples of risk-taking writing. Many thanks to Tirza Ben-Ezzer and Noah Gounoue for their digital expertise and brilliant artistry.

Many colleagues beyond Emory have supported this particular project with feedback on my writing or opportunities for talks, residencies, and publications: Jeremy Bendik-Keymer, Emma Bianchi, Paul Bové, Teagan Bradway, Kent Brintnall, Alex Brostoff, Morgane Cadieu, Niki Kasumi Clements, Penelope Deutscher, Michael Eng, James Faubion, Anne Garétta, Samir Haddad, Travis Holloway, Ryan Johnson, Rachel Jones, Mark Jordan, Annabel Kim, Kyoo Lee, Wendy Lochner, Ed McGushin, Elaine Miller, Laure Murat, Emily Parker, Mary Rawlinson, James Sares, Jana Sawicki, Stephen Seeley, Sidra Shahid, Robyn Wiegman, and Shannon Winnubst. Thank you all for nurturing the strangeness I was after. Lauren Guilmette, once my student but now more than ever the friend, colleague, and artist-philosopher I aspire to be: you know this book would not exist without you. Many thanks to philoSOPHIA for welcoming the experimental workshops Lauren and I have offered. Michelle LaPerrière, my dear childhood artist friend, never afraid to look the world's ugliness in the face, you teach me how to reshape all of it, the good and the bad, into something new. Thank you for all those days of art-making in Princeton and your stunning, inimitable example as an artist. Serene Jones: boundless gratitude for decades of walking, writing, and thinking together. And to my friends near and far (Chris, Debbie, Ren, Dianne, Amy, Donna, Megan, Leslie, Bill, Maxine), thank you. Many thanks to my friends in recovery, to my sanghas (Dilara, Michael, Chris, Nancy, Bobbi) for years of steady support, and to Shaila Catherine and the Barre Center for Buddhist Studies for a ten-month program on concentration practice that supported me in completing the book. I am grateful to all the artist-writer-teachers whose workshops taught me how to make new things (collages, altered books, cutouts, magical notebooks, fragmented text): Ellen Sheffield, Rebecca Goodale, Brenton Hamilton, Susan Niz, Leanne Dunic, and Shawn Sheehy.

Many thanks to the Brush Creek Foundation for the Arts, the Ragdale Foundation, and the Hambidge Center for residencies that offered time, a space to work, and the inspiration of other writers and artists. Special thanks to Jennifer Yorke, who first coaxed me onto the path of artists' books. I am grateful to Gabriel Rosenberg in Duke University's Department of Gender, Sexuality, and Feminist Studies for the invitation to give the Annual Queer Theory Lecture in honor of Eve Kosofsky Sedgwick, for allowing me to experiment with a lecture-installation in fragments. A special thank-you to Randall Johnson and Tim Isley for warm hospitality and philosophy talk during the Duke visit. Deep gratitude to Matthew Feliz, Carrie Robbins, and Alicia Walker at Bryn Mawr College for the three-day artist-philosopher residency that turned this book into an interactive, collaborative fragment extravaganza. Many thanks to Anette Fosner and Chuck Trettel at Colorchrome Atlanta for superb technical support with image scans and printing for installations. A deep bow of gratitude to Ryan Kendall for being the ideal editor, for patience and steady support, and for being the first one to say, "We'd like to publish this!"

So much of my past writing has circled around my mother. Here, again, the writing keeps wandering back to her. Thank you, Betsy McConnell, for the beautiful gift that is your life. And thanks beyond words to my entire family for your love, wisdom, laughter, Zoom calls, visits, and commitment to caring about the world. You have taught me how to stay with it—the writing, the making, the connecting—no matter what. Huge gratitude to my family—Beth, Lisi, Aston, Vivi, Gillian, John, Dad, Brooke—you continue to sustain me in ways large and small. To my life companion Tamara Jones: every day you make life luminescent. Thank you for your spirit, for your love, for your patience with my obsessions, for so graciously ducking beneath the fragments draped across our living space and tiptoeing around the scattered scraps of paper, onion skin, ribbons, and detritus on the floor. Thank you for so selflessly supporting a year of separation, for saying yes to my solitary immersion in fragments. Without that yes! I wouldn't have finished. Finally, I owe an inexpressible debt of gratitude to the late poet-philosopher Alexa Cucopulos. What she created during her short life will stay with me for the rest of mine. I dedicate *These Survivals* to her memory.